THE CONTINUING STORM

D1562857

In 2005 Hurricane Katrina crashed into the Gulf Coast and precipi-
tated the flooding of New Orleans. It was a towering catastrophe by any
standard. Some 1,800 persons were killed outright. More than a million
were forced to relocate, many for the remainder of their lives. A city of
500,000 was nearly emptied of life.

The Katrina Bookshelf is the result of a national effort to bring experts
together in a collaborative program of research on the human costs of
the disaster. The program was supported by the Ford, Gates, MacArthur,
Rockefeller, and Russell Sage Foundations and sponsored by the Social
Science Research Council (SSRC). This is the most comprehensive social
science coverage of a disaster to be found anywhere in the literature. It is
also a deeply human story.

THE CONTINUING STORM
LEARNING FROM KATRINA

KAI ERIKSON AND LORI PEEK

University of Texas Press

AUSTIN

Requests for permission to reproduce material from this work should be sent to:
Permissions
University of Texas Press
P.O. Box 7819
Austin, TX 78713-7819
utpress.utexas.edu/rp-form

∞ The paper used in this book meets the minimum requirements of
ANSI/NISO Z39.48-1992 (R1997) (Permanence of Paper).

Library of Congress Cataloging-in-Publication Data

Names: Erikson, Kai, 1931– author. | Peek, Lori A., author.
Title: The continuing storm : learning from Katrina / Kai Erikson and Lori Peek.
Other titles: Katrina bookshelf.
Description: First edition. | Austin : University of Texas Press, 2022. |
Series: The Katrina bookshelf | Includes bibliographical references and index.
Identifiers: LCCN 2021042949 (print) | LCCN 2021042950 (ebook)
ISBN 978-1-4773-2433-2 (hardcover)
ISBN 978-1-4773-2434-9 (paperback)
ISBN 978-1-4773-2435-6 (PDF ebook)
ISBN 978-1-4773-2436-3 (ePub ebook)
Subjects: LCSH: Hurricane Katrina, 2005—Social aspects. | Natural disasters—
Social aspects—United States. | Disasters—Social aspects—United States. |
Disaster victims—United States. | United States—Social conditions—21st century.
Classification: LCC HV636 2005.N4 E75 2022 (print) | LCC HV636 2005.N4 (ebook) |
DDC 363.34/9220976090511—dc23/eng/20220103
LC record available at https://lccn.loc.gov/2021042949
LC ebook record available at https://lccn.loc.gov/2021042950

doi:10.7560/324332

For Amanda, Bill, Bob, Brent, and Lynn

CONTENTS

PRELUDE

What we now call "Katrina" began as a weather pattern that took form out in the Atlantic. It started as an innocent puff of wind, grew into an ominous tropical storm, and then became a serious hurricane. When it was assigned a name, it had secured a place in meteorological history.

It became an event in *human* history when it entered Florida on the evening of August 25, 2005. It was a Category 1 hurricane at that point, with winds exceeding 75 miles per hour, the threshold used to distinguish tropical storms from hurricanes. It lost some of its momentum as it encountered the uneven surfaces of Florida—a rougher terrain to move across than the open sea had been—and it was demoted to the rank of tropical storm by the time it concluded its journey across that thin strip of land and entered the Gulf of Mexico. One hundred homes had been destroyed in Florida, damages were estimated in the hundreds of millions, and six persons had been killed, three by falling trees.[1] In the violent history of coastal storms, this one would have to be ranked as a fairly modest entry.

Katrina regained hurricane status not long after it entered the Gulf of Mexico on the western coast of Florida and returned to the smoother surface of the open waters. By August 27, it had become a Category 3 hurricane and was expanding rapidly in size and strength. It soon graduated from a Category 3 to a Category 5 hurricane, at which point the storm was generating sustained wind speeds well in excess of 156 miles per hour. Katrina was now on the verge of filling the entire Gulf with furious motion, reaching out some 200 miles in every direction from its center. The storm was alarmingly large by then, and it had become the strongest hurricane on record in the Gulf of Mexico. A buoy designed to measure the height of waves out in the Gulf brought news of some reaching 55 feet, the highest ever observed by scientists in that area.[2]

When Katrina landed on the Gulf Coast on the morning of August 29, it was a concentrated knot of fury, with winds lashing everything before it and immense tidal waves charging inland for miles. The damage to the natural landscape, the human settlements spread across it, and the people caught in its flow was beyond easy calculation. Towns along the Louisiana and Mississippi coasts were swept away altogether or crushed down into flat beds of debris by the force of the tidal surges. An early report portrayed the devastation everywhere: "The storm surge of Katrina struck the Mississippi coastline with such ferocity that entire coastal communities were obliterated, some left with little more than the foundations on which homes, businesses, government facilities, and other historical buildings once stood."[3]

It is easy to forget, given what we now know about the pain and misery soon to follow, how short the life span of the *hurricane* named Katrina actually was. Its fiercest winds abated within hours; its waters slipped back meekly into the Gulf within days. A huge amount of damage had been done, and the suffering it caused will last for generations. But the hurricane itself had disappeared from the radar. Its life was over.

In the early hours after Katrina made landfall, the people who had remained in New Orleans were looking out at a relatively calm August day, marveling at the fact that the epicenter of that dangerous spiral of wind had shifted slightly to the east at the last moment and spared them anything more than a harsh summer storm. Newspaper headlines were celebratory in their expressions of relief: "Hurricane Katrina Plows into Louisiana but Spares New Orleans Its Full Fury," declared one.[4] Another announced: "Last-Minute Shift Spares New Orleans Worst of Katrina."[5] The day after Katrina made landfall, the *New York Times* described New Orleans as having evaded the worst of it: "Hurricane Katrina pounded the Gulf Coast with devastating force at daybreak on Monday, sparing New Orleans the catastrophic hit that had been predicted."[6]

Residents who had decided to ride out the storm rather than evacuate and residents who had wanted to leave but could not find a way to arrange it exhaled a deep sigh of relief. The winds had done a noticeable amount of damage, and the levees on which the city depended so urgently were beginning to show signs of crumbling here and there. But the collapse that would soon take place was not yet fully apparent.

The *storm* we call "Katrina," then, was largely spent before the *flood* we call "Katrina" had reached its peak. They were two separate events, even if connected in obvious ways. As the world would soon see, those levees failed almost entirely, leaving 80 percent of New Orleans submerged under a dark, viscous depth of floodwater, with swollen human bodies facing downward and floating noiselessly on the surface. Tens of thousands of survivors were clustered together in what were then called "refuges of last resort," while thousands more were left stranded on rooftops, high sloping bridges, highway overpasses, and other elevated surfaces.

When Katrina roared over the horizon, it hit the coast with a sound that could be heard miles away. It then reached inland and scattered devastation over a stretch of land the size of Great Britain, its most prominent target being the city of New Orleans. It did an enormous amount of damage to the countryside it entered so abruptly, but it did even more harm to the bodies and minds and spirits of the people swept up in it.

Katrina crashed ashore more than a decade and a half ago. More recently, as the year 2019 gave way to 2020, an endless swarm of microscopic particles drifted over national borders without so much as a murmur. They were not only invisible to the human eye and inaudible to the human ear, but well beyond the range of the various instruments and devices we humans have invented over the years to sharpen our perception of the world around us. The Covid-19 pandemic that followed has caused an intense swell of death and illness across the human landscape and wrecked a countless number of lives.

It has been very hard for those of us submerged in the throes of the pandemic to visualize or conceptualize this new appearance on the global scene, to get a useful sense of its form and shape, to come to terms with it both literally and figuratively. That raises an important question. With these desperate circumstances pressing down so hard upon us now, why pay attention to an event like Hurricane Katrina that continues to recede ever further into the past? This new phenomenon feels so urgent, so overwhelming, so haunting.

There is an answer to that query, at least for present purposes. One of the most important objectives of sociologists and other social scientists is to describe events in such a way that they can serve as a kind of *lens* through which other investigators can get a useful perspective. That lens can provide an angle of vision on other events taking place, helping to bring into sharper focus their composition, their dimensions, and the trajectories they tend to follow as they make their way through time and space. The main reason why scientifically oriented researchers engage in these activities—and beyond any doubt the main reason why their efforts are supported by the larger social order—is to be better prepared for that inevitable event—the next time. A lens shaped in the past allows us to peer more intelligently at the present, and maybe even into the future.

We will be suggesting in this book that Katrina may well be the most *telling* disaster of our time, in the sense that it revealed so much about our society and the cultural climate in which we live. Severe disasters have an ability to tear away the outer surfaces of the social structures they slam into, showing what is going on down inside them in much the same way that a surgical procedure or an autopsy can cut through the outer layers of a body to provide a direct view of the workings of its inner organs.[7] A disaster like Katrina can tell us a great deal about the basic character of the American way of life in general.

The story of Katrina can be telling in another respect as well. If we look at it thoughtfully enough, it can help us determine what to concentrate on as perplexing new catastrophes confront us from afar or are generated within our midst. So we end this brief comment with an invitation to the reader to keep the pandemic that is so important a reality of the present in the back of your mind as you follow this account of Katrina. It is a compelling tale on its own, but it can also serve as a perceptual doorway into other realities. We will return to that thought as this book comes to its close.

The body of the text to follow, as the table of contents indicates, is divided into three parts and seven chapters. It closes with a postlude.

Part I consists of two chapters. The first offers an overview of what happened "Along the Shores of the Gulf" in the time of Katrina, and the second describes what happened "On the Streets of New Orleans." The second chapter is much longer than the first because in many ways the story of New Orleans became *the* story of Katrina, no matter how out of balance that may feel at first. For one thing, New Orleans was by many measures the worst casualty of that disaster in both the short term and the long term. For another, the suffering that was on full display on the streets of New Orleans became a national and even international symbol of urban poverty and racial injustice. And the "meaning" of Katrina was given narrative frame by the visiting media as well as by local and national leaders; as we detail in chapter 2, that framing had many consequences.

Part II, "Locating Katrina," is divided into two chapters entitled "In Time" and "In Space." That may seem like an odd set of inquiries at first glance. Chapter 3 asks when a disaster like Katrina can be said to have begun and when it can be said to have come to an end. How should it be located in time? Commentators generally mark the past-ness of disasters like Katrina by noting their anniversaries, and almost every account of the disaster known as Katrina—including the one we offer here in this prelude—opens with the fateful date of August 29, 2005. Thus, August 2015 was the tenth anniversary of Katrina, August 2025 will be the twentieth, and so on.

The *storm* we call Katrina—the weather event that gathered strength out in the Atlantic and made landfall on the shores of the Gulf—can reasonably be dated in that way. But a strong case can be made that the *disaster* we call Katrina—a different entity by any reasonable standard—should not. To trace that event back to its origins in time will draw us down into a more distant past. An equally strong case can be made that this way of reckoning the passing of time does not reflect the experiences of those persons who were caught in the harsh currents of Katrina. For many if not most of them, Katrina is a continuing event. The winds may have stilled, the floodwaters may have receded, and the terror of the moment may be reduced, but the memories that interrupt the flow of the day and the dreams that disrupt the quiet of the night are an ongoing reality. For them, the past is not yet.

We should pause for a moment to make an observation that will come up again in the pages to follow. Any disturbance that qualifies as a disaster should be envisioned in our mind's eye as an interaction—"collision" may be a better term—between a precipitating event and the human setting it lands on.[8] Atmospheric scientists usually measure the size of a disastrous incident by its strength: the velocity of a hurricane's winds, the height of its storm surges, the volume of its floodwaters. But other observers, including social scientists, measure the severity of a disaster by the amount of harm it does to the human beings and the human settlements in its path. If a massive cyclone that ranked near the top of every known measurement of intensity demolished an uninhabited island out in the Pacific Ocean, it would probably attract the attention of a few observant meteorologists, but it would almost certainly go unnoticed by everyone else, including other specialists in the study of disasters. It would not even earn a mention on the evening news.

Chapter 4 will shift from a reflection on the nature of disasters in *time* to one on the nature of disasters in *space*. It is obvious that Katrina landed on easily identified parcels of land and left them painfully scarred: counties named Hancock and Harrison, townships named Buras and Waveland, a city named New Orleans, a precinct known as the Lower Ninth Ward. Each of these sites has its own place on the official maps of the region. But a disaster lands on *people* as well as on *places*, leaving its mark on them as well. The debris of a crushed home on the shores of the Gulf or in the Lower Ninth Ward can be located on the map, but the crushed hopes and spirits of those who lived there were soon scattered hundreds and sometimes thousands of miles away. It was they who absorbed a considerable part of the assault, they who still carry a considerable number of the wounds. But how do we take them into account if our understanding of where Katrina hit its target is limited to the particular acreage it landed on? The bodies of people who no longer live in those places are still part of the space struck by Katrina. How should we include them in our reckoning? That thought becomes all the more relevant when the time comes to calculate the costs of an event like Katrina, and even more so in deciding how to disburse relief funds to those who were most damaged by it. Billions of dollars were distributed within that original confined space, but hardly any in the second. That will be the main topic of chapter 4.

Part III, "Katrina as Human Experience," has three chapters, each dealing with a different phase of that terrifying disaster—before, during, and after. Chapter 5, "Before: Seeking Out the Most Vulnerable," draws attention to the common observation that disasters charging toward us often seem to have an almost uncanny ability to seek out the poorest and the least-defended persons in their path, as if closing in on a target. That outcome, obviously, has far more to do with power imbalances and the way we humans locate ourselves on the surfaces of the earth than it does with the intention of incoming storms.[9] The dispossessed and mistreated suffer their fate because the social order has assigned them to living spaces where storms are most likely to land, where floodwaters are most likely to settle, where dwellings are most likely to collapse, where toxic wastes are most likely to be deposited, and so on. It often feels to the victims as though they have been treated as less worthy, even expendable, by the social order they are a part of, and when disaster strikes, it appears that they are also being treated as less worthy and more expendable by the natural order as well.

Chapter 6, "During: Being Battered by the Storm," as the title indicates, deals with what happened to those caught up in the track of the hurricane. It should go without saying that the people who had to endure the sharpest blows were those who did not have the resources necessary to get out of harm's way, and the vast majority of the most vulnerable were poor or African American or both. It almost seemed as if trauma was seeking out the already traumatized, as if harm was seeking out the already harmed.

The seventh and final chapter of the book, "After: The Pains of Displacement," is in many ways the most distressing of all. The poorest segments of the population were living with the greatest risk and were the most likely to have to confront the storm head-on. They were also the most likely to be sent out of town, often to unknown destinations, after the storm had calmed. Officials had few choices, given the severity of what had just happened, but it felt to many who were being shoved out the door that the city was clearing itself of human beings as well as material debris.

The persons who were displaced to distant places—some were sent as far away as Alaska and Maine—had to count on the goodwill and compassion of the residents of the locations they landed in. For a while at least, they were welcomed warmly. Those have to rank among the most truly humane moments of this otherwise grim tale. But the local people assumed that they were taking care of fellow human beings only for a time. As the crisis continued and it became more and more obvious that the leaders of New Orleans were in no hurry to welcome their fellow townspeople home, local compassion began to fade. What came to be called "Katrina fatigue" set in, and the cruelest blow of all was soon to come.[10] Officials of the evacuees' home turf, the place they came from and belonged to, the ground in which their roots and those of all their kin had been planted for generations, simply did not want them back, ever. They had left the city temporarily in a time of peril but were now being treated as if they were exiles whose absence was a blessing.

The postlude to the book offers reflections on the current pandemic and discusses the ways in which the study of disasters like Katrina can help us to see and make better sense of other disasters. Such events have become an inescapable fact of our age, although disasters now do a good deal more damage than was once the case because of how we humans have spread ourselves out across space and ventured into ever more dangerous terrains. It is probably fair to say that we, residents of the so-called developed world, are at heart a restless and often reckless lot, charging into the future with chemicals we are not sure of the effects of, weapons we are not sure how to control, and technologies we are not really sure how to rein in, and yet with a feeling that we are rulers of the natural environment we find ourselves in and the built environment we construct all around us. In a sense, then, disasters have become our way of learning when we have gone too far. We tend to hurtle ahead at full throttle until we realize with a start that we have just bolted across that invisible line that marks the outer limits of our competence and capability.[11] We can reach into the past for striking examples to illustrate the point—Chernobyl, Bhopal, and the *Exxon Valdez* oil spill, to name a few. Katrina has now joined them as an example of our human urge to tempt fate and of the dire consequences that follow, especially for the most vulnerable among us.

A HURRICANE KNOWN AS KATRINA

ALONG THE SHORES OF THE GULF

All hell broke loose in the early morning of August 29, 2005, along the coasts of Louisiana, Mississippi, and Alabama. Hurricane Katrina had been brewing out in the warm waters of the Gulf of Mexico for several days by then, almost as if it had paused for a moment to test its winds and flex its muscles for the task ahead. Once ready, Katrina lunged ashore, leveling human settlements in its path. And then, moments later, the hurricane's vigor not yet spent, it drove further inland.

Katrina shifted directions a bit as it approached the Gulf Coast, giving many people in New Orleans the momentary feeling that they had been spared. Katrina's new targets became the shores of Hancock County and Harrison County in the western portions of Mississippi via Plaquemines and St. Bernard Parishes—the Louisiana coastal parishes south of New Orleans—and St. Tammany Parish on the north shore of Lake Pontchartrain. Coastal towns like Bay St. Louis, Buras, Pass Christian, Waveland, and parts of Biloxi were annihilated by Katrina, first by the winds and then by the storm surges, some of which approached 30 feet in height. One observer said that "it was as if a large rake had come through the area and pulled these small Gulf towns into the Gulf of Mexico, leaving behind only slab foundations or, in some cases, nothing at all."[1] President George W. Bush described the damage as "worse than imaginable." He continued: "It's as if the entire Gulf Coast were obliterated by the worst kind of weapon you can imagine."[2] The governor of Mississippi, Haley Barbour, announced flatly: "The 80 miles across the Mississippi Gulf Coast is largely destroyed. A town like Waveland, Mississippi, has no inhabitable structures—none."[3]

Damages ranged along the coastline in either direction of that Mississippi epicenter for hundreds of miles, deep into Louisiana to the west and into Alabama and the Florida panhandle to the east. When those thrusts of water had done their work along the shore, they charged as many as six miles inland on hard land surfaces and as many as twelve miles inland along openings like rivers and bays. Jan Moller, writing for the *New Orleans Times-Picayune*, described what the eye could see from above:

> Metal buildings twisted beyond recognition. Neighborhoods almost completely destroyed and submerged, the only clue that humans once lived there being the telephone lines that rise above the floodwaters.
>
> If anyone here in the southeast tip of Louisiana stayed behind and tried to weather Hurricane Katrina as she bulldozed her way north, there was no sign of them Tuesday morning during a three-hour aerial tour of the fishing and farming villages at the mouth of the Mississippi River.
>
> Seen from 1,200 feet above, Katrina left a scene of near-total devastation. Houses and businesses that weren't shattered by the wind were submerged in several feet of water where the river flooded its banks. The only sign of life were a few stray cattle that clung to what little firm ground remained, and the rescue boats searching for anyone who might have been foolish enough to think they could withstand the storm.
>
> Empire. Buras. Triumph. Boothville. Venice. The farther south and east one flies above what used to be La. 23, the deeper the water gets and the more total the destruction. While homes sit underwater, fishing boats lie scattered about like flotsam, presumably deposited there by high winds and storm surge.[4]

Gross figures can offer no more than a remote sense of the enormity of the damage done to that devastated landscape. It has been estimated, for example, that the storm completely destroyed or made uninhabitable 300,000 houses along the coast.[5] That amounts to well over a million persons left without a home. It washed away hundreds of essential bridges and overpasses and left thousands of equally essential roadways impassable for long stretches of time, isolating any number of badly damaged communities from outside emergency services. More than three million customer phone lines were knocked down in affected parts of the Gulf Coast at a time when desperate victims of the storm most badly needed not only help but news of what was happening to family members and other loved ones elsewhere.

The damage done by Katrina to the *natural* landscape is impossible to estimate for the obvious reason that its effects will not be known fully until well into the future. But there were ominous signs of persisting trouble there. In a few hours, as we note again later in this account, Katrina wiped out 36 square miles of Louisiana wetlands, which for millennia had been nature's way of protecting the terrains further inland against disturbances issuing from the open sea.[6] Katrina was also responsible for ten oil spills, which collectively spewed a volume of petroleum into the environment larger than some of the worst spills on record in the United States.[7] The oil dumped into the region's waterways in those few hours came to more than two-thirds of the amount poured out in the *Exxon Valdez* oil spill of 1989. Katrina ultimately caused the second-largest oil spill in the history of the United States. That distinction was erased from the record book five years later by the 2010 Deepwater Horizon oil spill.[8] Still, Hurricane Katrina remains a major contributor to the spoiling of the natural surround. One can add to that dismal account that Katrina slammed into and compromised hundreds of facilities that handled dangerous chemicals, including more than thirty hazardous waste sites.[9] The long-term costs of these additional disasters may never be fully known.

Scenes of such vast desolation often defy easy comprehension, lying beyond our normal ability to see, to sense, even to imagine what it all means as human experience. How can one convey that amount of destruction in a few sentences of inert words spread out on the printed page, all of them phrased in the past tense? Some 1,800 people dead from the storm itself. Hundreds of thousands of dwellings flattened. More than a million persons without proper shelter, electricity, or running water. How might one get some measure of what that devastation must have been like for persons who were immersed in it and lived through it? What did it look like, and feel like?

A group of us traveled to Mississippi and Louisiana not long after the storm, trying to capture a sense of it all through field notes and photographs of that devastated landscape. A snapshot, of course, can offer only a stationary, silent reflection of what had to have been a tremendous explosion of sound and motion. Still, those early days in the field offered a hint.

What the eye could see and the camera could record—at ground level this time—were large swaths of land scraped clean along the shoreline, with just enough bits of wreckage strewn about to confirm that these areas had once been comfortable, settled neighborhoods. Entire communities, now left uninhabitable, had been totally abandoned. The original locations of the destroyed homes of the former residents were marked by the concrete slabs on which they had been built. Brick steps ascended to nowhere, cruel reminders of where houses had once firmly stood.

FIGURE 1.1. An upended house and steps to nowhere along
the US Gulf Coast. Photo © Lori Peek, 2006.

If you looked away from the shoreline and into interior areas, you could see stacks of debris, some of them containing the splintered remains of structures that had been picked up near the shore in their entirety by the storm surge and slammed, like battering rams, into other structures fifty paces inland. It was a dizzying sight: A car, crushed to the ground, its dead headlights peering out like blank eyes from under a vast pile of rubble. Large homes picked up whole by the surge and deposited further inland, the roof that once sheltered the interior serving as the surface on which it now crumpled. Refrigerators sitting apart from the splintered remains of the buildings that may once have housed them, their doors wide open and their contents spilled out all over the visible surfaces of the wreckage. Pieces of living room furniture strewn atop the walls that once protected them. Scraps of clothing, much of it underwear, fluttering overhead from the branches of trees in a soft post-Katrina breeze.

It was almost as if the storm surges of Katrina had mocked our sense of what belongs inside and what outside, what is private and what public. The very order of life seemed to have been turned inside out and upside down too.

Those tree branches overhead were worthy of attention. Many of the trees, some with leaves still hanging on, stood intact in spaces where every human-built structure around them had been flattened, providing an ironic reminder of the difference between human architecture and natural architecture. Their round trunks give trees a shape that allows surges of water to flow around them, and their branches are flexible enough to bend with the harshest of winds. Compare those features to those of one-, two-, or three-story buildings, which are built with nothing but flat surfaces that winds cannot circle around. Moreover, along most American seashores, buildings are constructed with one of the most vulnerable of those surfaces deliberately facing the exact location from which the winds and waters are most likely to charge ashore head-on. That's the water view.

What the eye can see, and the camera can record, give us some sense of the effects of a disaster like Katrina, but these are really just glances into an almost endless milieu. The sight of a house crushed into a mound of debris may stick in the mind, but news of 100,000 crushed houses has a way of receding into a gray statistical blur.

Another way to get a sense of the human experience of Katrina is to listen to persons who experienced the devastation firsthand—an approach used widely, if sporadically, by journalists and more systematically by researchers. When we read through a large collection of the personal narratives published in the media and by our fellow social scientists, what becomes clear is the utter sense of disorientation that people felt in the immediate aftermath of Katrina. One resident of Buras, a small rural community in lower Louisiana, tried to convey what it felt like to see everything gone: "I knew I was on the right street, but I kept looking around, turning around, searching for the things I knew should be there....I must have looked like a dog chasing my own tail."[10] Another resident described the effect of the disintegration of familiar surrounds this way: "I got lost, and there is only one road. I have lived here my whole life."[11]

Residents of coastal communities searched desperately for familiar landmarks: a church steeple, a child's school building, a home. These structures help situate people. They are the anchors of our social worlds. After Katrina, people were left feeling unmoored because many such places were either blown away or so badly damaged that they were unrecognizable. Local residents had to turn to other means to find their way: "We went to the library, and we brought [a website] up, which gave you the satellite picture and you could go to it and you could see. You go to this location, there's nothing there. You go to that location, there's nothing there."[12]

The stories of those who returned to homes that had remained upright after the winds subsided and the water retreated back into the Gulf of Mexico were no less dreadful. A man from a small village on the east bank of the Mississippi River, located in Plaquemines Parish, trudged through mud several inches thick to survey his property. His two-story brick house had withstood Katrina's fury. But, as a reporter recounted, "it was all but hidden from view by the remains of a wooden house that had wrapped around a tree in his front yard." The man told the journalist, "This house in my yard, I don't even know who owns it. I can't even recognize it as one of my neighbor's." The reporter picked up the description from there:

> Winds clocked at upwards of 100 miles per hour had torn the bricks off the back of [his] house and stripped almost all the leaves off the trees in his yard. A massive tidal surge had burst through his front door and upended everything inside, reaching half-way up the walls of the house's second floor before receding.[13]

For anyone traveling along the torn and scarred landscape of the Gulf Coast, an undamaged home was an uncommon sight after Katrina made landfall. Trailers were overturned or completely blown away. Boats were pitched far from the water. Church steeples lay on the ground, bearing mute witness to the power of Katrina's lashing winds.

To understand the effects of Katrina on the people of the coastal lands—particularly the people of the Louisiana wetlands—it is useful to know something of their way of life. We will not venture into that cultural domain in any detail now, but it should be noted that they live in what has been described as both the most fragile and most productive ecosystem in North America.[14]

This ecosystem is *fragile* in the sense that the land is made up entirely of bits of silt carried southward by the Mississippi River over thousands of years from regions as far north as Minnesota, as far west as the Rocky Mountains, and as far east as the Appalachian Mountains. Those deposits tend to be soft underfoot and subject to periodic shifts as the Mississippi and all the other waterways it brings into being—channels, estuaries, deltas, bayous—rearrange the contour of the land itself. Stretches of marshland can reach 50 miles or more inland from the coastline. Vast portions of those wetlands are simply dissolving as the waters of the sea reach into and take over what was once solid land. Maps of the region portray the coastline as a crisp borderline drawn across space, with waters tinted blue on one side of that divide. But to seagulls flying overhead, there is no clear shoreline. The water gradually yields to land across an intermediate mixture that is neither for miles.

The ecosystem is *productive* in the sense that a large proportion of the seafood consumed in the United States comes from coastal Louisiana: shrimp, oysters, blue crab, yellowfin tuna, red snapper, mullet.[15]

Generations of Gulf Coast residents have made their livelihoods through the bountiful waters of the region. A distinctive way of life has emerged among the sturdy people who regard these fertile terrains as their natural *place*, their *niche*, their *home-land*. That way of life reflects a deep feeling that they belong to the habitat surrounding them in almost the same way that the creatures they harvest do. They feel grounded there. Irish country people of an earlier time were known to say that "their name is on the land"—that land being the particular plot of soil they lived on and cultivated. The people of these coastal lands, in contrast, are rooted to their habitat in that they drift with the natural flow of the region. They range across the land and the water by foot, by boat, or by standing still as their harvests float by. A considerable number of these residents, moreover, have reason to suppose that they are living in the same location and sharing the same prospects as generations of their ancestors.

The fragility of the land combines with their deep attachment to it to make them quite vulnerable and exposed when hurricanes come across the horizon and slam into the coastlands. But they also have a considerable store of experience and knowledge to draw on in such times of danger, and for the most part they return, restore, reclaim, and then brace for the next time. One longtime resident of Plaquemines Parish in Louisiana, a native of those parts and also a coordinator of an important restoration project located there, sent out reports highlighting that resiliency a few days after Katrina struck the Gulf Coast:

> I want to help you understand our people....
>
> People not from here love this region because we are so different. And we are different because our culture has remained intact. Our people do not leave this place. We have been here for generations.... Our connection to our wetlands is too strong for us to be content anywhere else. Our way of life was born out of these wetlands, and we have maintained that connection. Those wetlands are the clothing around our communities. They protect our homes and they are symbols as well as the source of who we are.
>
> One family of shrimpers we hauled out of Grand Isle...was an inspiration to me. These people lost everything but the clothes they were wearing and their boat. I noticed that the children—they were of adult age—began to sob as we passed the destruction of camps and homes on the side of the road.... [But] the patriarch, the shrimper, a man who knew nothing else but the adventurous life of a commercial shrimper

was just beaming—a big old smile. And he said to me, "Hey, we're going to get over this. We're going to do what we always do. We're going to help each other until we get back on our feet. That's what we do down here."

Our somewhat isolated settlement pattern served to separate communities from one another, especially before the advent of the modern highway system, but it also kept us firmly connected to the bayous as a source of livelihood and recreation.

Bert is from lower Plaquemines Parish. He and his wife stayed at my house for a night over the weekend. In such a sparsely populated parish, everyone knows everyone else, so I have always known his family. [His people] are oystermen and they have been so for generations. Hard-working people like that are many on the bayou. Bert's house was washed away by the storm surge from Katrina. We were on my patio, talking about the future of our region. I was wearing a t-shirt imprinted with a BACK TO THE BAYOU paddle-trip logo. I asked: "What are you going to do, Bert?" He pointed to my shirt and said: "I'm going back to the bayou. I have to."[16]

It is important to appreciate that the people of the Gulf Coast experienced a very different type of disaster than the people of New Orleans did.[17] Residents of the coast took it for granted that they had been victims of a *natural* event surging in from a distant place, while the people of New Orleans shared a sense that they had been victims of stunning failures in human engineering and, far more to the point, in human *caring*. The two events took place at the same time and are known by the same code name, Katrina, but they belong to different universes. This matters for at least two reasons.

First, the people of the Gulf Coast tended to experience Katrina as one of a continuing sequence of similar events, one of the costs of living in a vulnerable part of the world. Katrina was understood to have been one of the worst on record, if not the worst; nevertheless, it was preceded by other hurricanes with widely remembered names (Audrey, Camille, Betsy, Andrew), and it was soon to be followed by others with now equally familiar names (Rita, Harvey, María, Ida). The people on the Gulf Coast who found themselves in the path of Katrina suffered deep and lasting wounds, no question about that, but at the same time they had experienced such events before and felt that they, like the shrimper and the oysterman described earlier, had no real choice but to return. The bayou was home. It was where they belonged and where many of them, although certainly not all, would be going back to as soon as the fates allowed.[18] In that sense, Katrina had been a natural fact of everyday life, a persistent reality like the change of seasons. A reporter put it well in suggesting that "they live forever with recovery." The people of New Orleans, however, were experiencing something quite different. Few there took Katrina to be wholly an act of nature.[19] Most residents of the city regarded it as an act of human negligence, if not one of outright malice.

Second, individuals who have a hard time recovering from the effects of what they take to be a "natural disaster" have an easier time of it than people who have to cope with the reality that the attack on them came not from the natural world, but from the social world in which they participate.[20] It is increasingly well understood among those who study human disasters that the traumatic effects that follow the realization that one cannot rely on the *human* world any more than the *natural* world can be emotionally as well as spiritually devastating. To feel that one has been caught unaware in a natural catastrophe is far easier to live with than to feel that one has been deeply damaged by the miscalculations or the indifference of fellow human beings—all the more so if those human beings belong to the same community or in some other way are supposed to have one's best interests at heart. So in that respect, too, there is a marked difference between the "Katrina" that struck the coast and the "Katrina" that flooded New Orleans.

We turn now to the principal focus of the rest of the book—what happened to the people of New Orleans after Katrina hit home. One of the clearest aspects of the media coverage of Katrina was the almost fierce intensity of the national spotlight turned on the city of New Orleans, even though the disaster had raged over a much larger span of land. New Orleans is where a good part of the damage and a considerable majority of the deaths occurred, to be sure, but at the same time it was immensely convenient to the press to be able to concentrate its attention on what was already a widely known, even iconic, city.[21] At times, it almost seemed as though the drama of Katrina had been compressed so as to fit on a smaller and more easily contained stage. In a way, we risk doing the same thing here by drawing attention to what happened in the city of New Orleans. But there are lessons to be learned from what unfolded in the city, lessons that underscore why Katrina still stands as one of the most *revealing* disasters in our national experience.

ON THE STREETS OF NEW ORLEANS

In the hours before Hurricane Katrina slammed into the mainland, meteorologists were almost unanimous in predicting that the storm had taken direct aim at New Orleans and that serious trouble was afoot. But as we noted earlier, Katrina underwent a sudden shift of trajectory and set its sights a degree or two eastward. For a fleeting moment, it seemed that the city had been spared.

It soon became apparent, however, that those hopeful early reports were entirely off the mark. As it turned out, newscasters were looking in the wrong direction and paying attention to the wrong indicators. They had focused their binoculars to the south, which was where the storm was expected to land and where the assault on New Orleans was expected to begin. They simply did not notice that the heavy winds and rains that usually precede hurricanes had already begun their harsh project to the north—literally behind their backs—where Lake Pontchartrain forms the upper boundary of New Orleans. So Katrina had not yet made landfall on the coast when the levees protecting New Orleans from the waters to their north began to crumble.[1] The torrents of lake water that rushed through those open gaps, in turn, threatened the levees and floodwalls that were built to protect the canals and other waterways that had been sliced through the city by engineers years ago.

Before long, flooding had spread across a considerable part of New Orleans, largely unnoticed by newscasters. Journalists were receiving fragments of news and even video of what was happening around them from colleagues who had ventured out into the field, but they seemed unsure about how to insert them into upcoming broadcasts. On the evening of August 29, for example, Fox News actually interrupted its Katrina coverage from the heart of New Orleans to inform its listeners about a flood taking place in Santiago, Chile, that had reached 10 *inches* above street level.

It was as if they were unaware that floodwaters reaching 10 to 20 *feet* above street level were gathering less than a mile away.[2]

So the *flood* known as Katrina was well under way on that morning of August 29. It poured into St. Bernard Parish, expanded into New Orleans East, and then moved ahead with increasing confidence into the Lower Ninth Ward. It soon reached 80 percent of the city and would not fully disappear for weeks.

For a period following Katrina, one could visit neighborhoods where the floodwaters had remained after reaching their highest point and before receding. Most of the moldering structures in these neighborhoods were clearly marked with horizontal lines that looked like bathtub rings, indicating where the water had settled for a while. If you stood near one of those lines, you recognized, with a shudder, that everything you could see at eye level in every direction had been underwater not very long before. Very few of us have ever looked at, or even imagined, flood scenes except from vantage points above them. What we would have seen had we been down in that darkness was a thick mixture of floodwater and an almost endless tonnage of sewage and debris and waste of all kinds—some of it toxic—as well as the bloated bodies of rodents and household pets and other creatures that had learned over time to live in human settlements. And of course, the news that finally reached viewers was that a sickening number of corpses in that water overhead turned out to be human.

A brief comment about the geography of New Orleans. It is one of the nation's most important port cities, the place where water traffic moving south from ports along the Mississippi River meets water traffic moving north from the Gulf of Mexico. On simplified maps of the United States, the Mississippi is represented as a fairly steady flow of water from north to south. But one part of the river, especially when it enters the southland, makes its way in wide, easy curves as it adjusts to and shapes the contours of the land it passes through. On more detailed maps of the southern region, then, the Mississippi River is represented as moving from west to east as it takes one of those curves across the stretch of land that now contains New Orleans. Thus, the city itself is sandwiched between two large bodies of water: Lake Pontchartrain to the north and the Mississippi River to the south.

A good portion of the land in between is shaped like a shallow basin, much of it consisting of drained wetlands, which are vulnerable to both the waters that loom above the city and those that loom below it. For the most

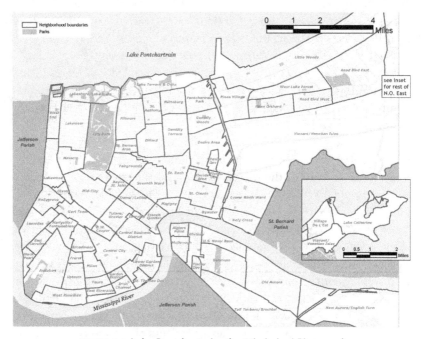

FIGURE 2.1. Lake Pontchartrain, the Mississippi River, and neighborhoods in Orleans Parish and surrounding areas. Used with permission. Copyright © 2004 The Data Center, www.datacenterresearch.org.

part, New Orleans is shielded from the Mississippi by levees constructed by the work of human hands.

Before Katrina, it was well understood that more than half of New Orleans was situated below sea level, as defined by the waters of the Gulf. But Katrina soon made clear that almost the entire city, when unprotected by levees, was vulnerable to the waters of a restless, roiled lake above it and the river system rolling through it. As one observer suggested, drawing on a vocabulary local to the New Orleans area, the city is "a true super bowl," and it is sinking up to two inches a year.[3] Given the level and scope of the inundation, some of the only dry ground to be seen from the air was a mile-wide curve of land along the Mississippi—the real Crescent City in full view. It is there that most tourists gather, and it was there that the media set up their central offices after Katrina.

The early settlers of what would become New Orleans had to quickly figure out how to live with the complex hand that nature dealt to the region. The settlers who owned land developed a spotty patchwork levee system of uneven quality that provided inconsistent protection. In more recent times, when "progress" and "profit" so indelibly worked their way into American thinking, a newer breed of settler began to rearrange the landscape dramatically to "improve on" the ways of nature.[4] In New Orleans, that meant carving a whole lacery of waterways through the city.

The most important shipping lanes over the long term were the Industrial Canal—which reached north from the Mississippi River to Lake Pontchartrain and was made possible by the invention of locks in the nineteenth century—and then, once that was accomplished, the Mississippi River Gulf Outlet, which stretched from New Orleans all the way south to the Gulf of Mexico. This shipping lane was soon better known by its initials, MRGO, which became, irresistibly, "Mr. Go" to the local people. Ivor van Heerden, a marine scientist and hurricane expert, would later call this channel "an excellent storm surge delivery system"; in other words, the MRGO provided a truly efficient way for the raging waters of the Gulf to reach inland and do their harm many miles to the north in stormy times.[5] Dan Baum, a local writer, described in *The New Yorker* the combined action of the Industrial Canal and Mr. Go during Katrina:

> The two waterways funneled Katrina's surge into a wedge that burst the Industrial Canal's levee with a sound like cannon fire early in the morning of August 29....Not a house in the Lower Nine was spared; most of those which didn't collapse or slide off their foundations flooded to their rooflines.[6]

We mention those engineering projects now for two reasons. The first is that they will figure prominently in the chapter on locating Katrina in time. The second is to emphasize the important point that the flooding of New Orleans owed most of its size and most of its lethal force to human-built structures within the city itself. A "natural" disaster it most surely was not.[7]

We should also add a note here about the demography—or what is also sometimes called the "social geography"—of New Orleans. The metropolitan region itself, to oversimplify a bit, can be divided into three different parcels: the elevated crescent along the Mississippi River, the sunken bowl that makes up so much of New Orleans, and the suburbs that spread out from that center in all directions. Those persons who chose to and those who could afford to move out to the suburbs in the second half of the twentieth century were largely White, while those who remained in the central city were largely Black.[8] The same White flight pattern was emerging elsewhere across the nation in sharp and bitter reaction to court-ordered racial desegregation efforts, particularly those involving public schools. New Orleans hit its population peak in 1960 with some 627,525 residents, but large-scale abandonment of the city followed as an astonishing 70,000 White residents left the central city in the 1960s and 90,000 more in the 1970s.[9]

That steady tide outward drawing wealthier Whites away from the city helped generate the concentration of poverty and misfortune that so clearly characterized central New Orleans at the time of Katrina's landfall. The public schools by then were 94 percent Black, and 80 percent of the students were poor enough to meet eligibility requirements for free lunch or reduced-cost lunch subsidies.[10] In August 2005, the Crescent City had a poverty rate of 23 percent, which was nearly twice the national average at the time.[11] Black residents were strapped by incomes that were 40 percent less than those earned by Whites.[12] In fact, the disparity between the well-off and the poor in central New Orleans was among the worst in the country.[13] Beyond those striking disadvantages, however, the rearrangement of the population made African American residents of New Orleans even more susceptible to the effects and aftereffects of disaster than their relative poverty would have suggested because so many of their homes were, quite literally, underwater.

On Tuesday, August 30, one day after the hurricane made landfall and the floodwaters entered New Orleans, the media had little choice but to recognize that they had been wrong. They had been outwitted by the sly maneuvers of Katrina working behind their backs, and so they quickly turned their attention to the perils being faced by survivors. Tens of thousands of people, visibly stranded on elevated surfaces, most without food or clean water or protection from the fierce August sun, were signaling skyward and looking outward for organized rescue efforts that were slow to arrive or absent altogether.

Meanwhile, tens of thousands more people were making their way through the floodwaters to public shelters like the Superdome and the Convention Center. These places of refuge, now filling up with sweltering crowds of people, had little in the way of lighting, no air-conditioning, no functioning water or sewer systems, and an increasingly putrid odor. The civil rights leader Rev. Jesse Jackson, upon visiting the Convention Center at a time when close to twenty thousand persons, almost all of them African American, were crammed together, said that the place "looks like the hull of a slave ship."[14] Days after Katrina made landfall, crowds of survivors waited in the broiling sun for transport from the Convention Center and the Superdome.

FIGURE 2.2. Katrina survivors await aid and evacuation assistance.
Photo © Charlie Varley/varleypix.com, 2005.

The people of New Orleans had been ordered to evacuate the city, but anyone familiar with the demography of New Orleans had to have known that this was not a possibility for a considerable portion of the population. To evacuate, a person would need access to a working motor vehicle, since no public transportation was being offered, and making a go of it away from home would require credit cards or cash on hand. Evacuating also required having some idea of how to navigate unfamiliar social terrain. A fifty-seven-year-old woman who was unable to leave in advance of an earlier storm that threatened New Orleans said of all such orders to evacuate: "Got no place to go and no way to get there," she said. "They say to evacuate, but they don't say how I'm supposed to do that. If I can't walk it or get there on a bus, I don't go. I don't got a car. My daughter don't either."[15]

That woman and her daughter were not alone. Somewhere between one-quarter and one-fifth of New Orleans families did not own a vehicle when Katrina roared ashore, never mind a reliable one with a tank full of gas.[16] Moreover, it is difficult enough for a nuclear family of four or five who live in the same household to gather necessities for a trip out of town and then evacuate in the family car. But it is something else entirely for an extended family that includes three or four generations scattered over a number of different dwelling places—a far more likely arrangement for

Black families in Louisiana. In fact, according to the sociologist Elizabeth Fussell, Louisiana, compared to the rest of the nation, is home to more people who were born and raised there; as a consequence, most of their social networks are also deeply rooted and tightly interwoven in place.[17] The sentiment of one twenty-three-year-old Katrina survivor was shared by thousands: "I've been in New Orleans all my life. All my family was born and raised in New Orleans.... That is where we are from."[18]

It should be added that individuals who elected to ride out the storm at home rather than evacuate on the theory that they knew how to survive such emergencies were, ironically, quite right in their calculations. They had been warned that a dangerous hurricane might reach up from the Gulf, not that the city's levee system might collapse and drown the city. That fearful storm never did hit New Orleans head-on. Secretary of Homeland Security Michael Chertoff, the official in charge of the federal response to Katrina, said afterward: "The critical thing was to get people out before the disaster. Some people chose not to obey that order. That was a mistake on their part."[19] What happened next was their own fault, he was very clearly saying.

The fact is that Chertoff could hardly have been more mistaken: those who remained were quite right to think that they could survive the storm surging upward from the south. The first "critical thing" had been for his agency to appreciate and then anticipate the dangers posed by the city's inadequate levee system, and the second was for that agency to come up with ways to help ill-equipped residents safely evacuate from the city.[20] The federal government became responsible for making these efforts once local and state efforts were so visibly overwhelmed, but it almost entirely ignored this responsibility. It also ignored the lessons derived from previous disaster planning exercises that had foreshadowed many of Katrina's worst impacts.[21]

Looking over the devastated landscape—bodies floating in rank water, families stuck on rooftops signaling for rescue, vast numbers of people pressed together in impossible squalor—newscasters began to wonder about that failure of the federal response. Around 100,000 citizens of a rich country were in desperate need of help, and yet, so far, nothing at all had happened. Thousands of prisoners were left shackled and alone in their cells during Katrina, and hospitals and nursing homes were left full.[22] Medical assistance was virtually nonexistent, with unknown numbers left dead or dying as a consequence.[23]

Print media almost ran out of ways to convey what the damaged scene looked like, felt like, and smelled like. Nancy Gibbs, writing in *Time* magazine, wondered "whether the storm of '05 will be remembered mainly as the worst natural disaster in our history or the worst response to a disaster in our history. Or both."[24] Either way, she concluded, "the treatment of the living, Black and poor and old and sick, was a disgrace."[25] Among the experts to whom the media frequently turned for advice on this matter was Enrico Quarantelli, a veteran scholar of disaster research. Katrina was "the worst mishandled disaster" he was aware of, he said, in a lifetime of studying them.[26]

As the designated leaders of the response were trying to figure out how to respond, dozens of fires fueled by ruptured gas lines broke out across New Orleans. The city was now "tormented by plagues of flame as well as flood" as fires burned unchecked or were fought by helicopters "dropping buckets of water from the Mississippi."[27] Neither the scene itself nor the federal response to it was encouraging by any measure.

It is worth pointing out, however, that the reaction of local residents was truly notable, a lasting credit to the generosity and gallantry of the people of New Orleans and surrounding areas. Tricia Wachtendorf and James M. Kendra, longtime researchers of disasters, emphasize that Katrina survivors proved themselves to be remarkably well skilled in the art of improvisation.[28] In the absence of any serious sign of federal assistance, the city's residents found ways to save each other.

Formal rescue efforts began with local units of the Coast Guard. Their efforts also qualify as improvisation in that, without waiting for federal or other directives, they were responding to the emergency on the basis of insights informed by knowledge of the milieu. Estimates suggest that well over twenty thousand people were rescued by the Coast Guard, largely by helicopter, and many of them owe their lives to that effort.[29]

The Louisiana Department of Wildlife and Fisheries, operating in the same spirit, was credited with also saving large numbers of people, mostly by boat.[30] One of the game wardens with the department described what he and his colleagues witnessed when they arrived in the city: "When we got to the top of the bridge and looked across, everything below there—the Lower Ninth Ward toward St. Bernard Parish—was just one big lake. There were people sitting on their roofs yelling for help. We could hear others hammering on their roofs from inside their attics. It was just a sight I'll never forget." Pausing for a moment, he continued, "We immediately started launching our boats and rescuing the living."[31]

Official reports suggest that by week's end the Louisiana Department of Wildlife and Fisheries, supported by volunteer game wardens who had traveled from as far away as Canada to contribute to the rescue efforts, had

FIGURE 2.3. A boat arrives to rescue a man who cut through his rooftop from inside with an ax to escape the floodwaters rising to his attic. Photo © Charlie Varley/varleypix.com, 2005.

moved about twenty-one thousand residents in the New Orleans metropolitan area from the floodwaters to higher ground.[32] "We are picking up as many people as the boats can hold," the secretary of Wildlife and Fisheries said, "and we have others hanging on the sides."[33]

While these first responders were hard at work, a large number of able-bodied survivors who were already *inside* the city and had access to canoes, rowboats, or other serviceable watercraft focused on saving people in their own neighborhoods or nearby ones. They moved through the murky waters in an attempt to offer relief to the most vulnerable.[34] Meanwhile, a virtual armada of additional small boat craft, hitched to pickup trucks or lashed on top of them, was progressing toward the zone of trouble. Those from *outside* the city made a considerable difference as well. Louisiana is a land of estuaries, bayous, and ever-shifting rivers. Its residents know the ways of water. As these volunteer groups grew in size, they came to be called the "Cajun Navy" or the "Cajun Flotilla."

We will never know how many stranded people were saved by volunteers who took the risk of entering New Orleans for search-and-rescue purposes. Reliable sources suggest that perhaps as many as ten thousand people were rescued by a number of heroic men and women in the early days after Katrina.[35] Nor will we ever know what the eventual size of that volunteer armada would have grown to if the local and federal authorities—fearing that those visitors were coming to the city with the evil intent of looting—had not set up road blockades to stop their entrance.[36] Government officials literally prevented volunteers from rescuing stranded survivors.

THE MEDIA FINDS A FOCUS

The early days of the media's response to the arrival of Katrina in New Orleans can be divided into three vastly oversimplified phases. The first day, August 29, was a time of denial: most people were unable to comprehend or find an appropriate frame for what the unaided eye could plainly see out there on the streets. On the second day, August 30, the media, accepting the obvious, began to report with considerable vigor on the sad state of the city and its many stranded residents; as the day lengthened, they became more and more astonished, and more and more appalled, at the absence of federal support. As the second day gave way to the third and then the fourth, however, the media abruptly shifted in focus and began to offer a far more ominous view of what was happening on those streets.

That shift began with reports of widespread looting throughout the city. At first, that news felt like familiar territory, both to experienced members of the press and to specialists in the study of disasters, because rumors of looting are known to be fairly common in these moments, even though they are usually found to be obvious exaggerations.[37] Such rumors are generally written off quickly, although they often persist.

But New Orleans is a more volatile, more racially divided place than most of the smaller and more homogenous communities that find themselves in the path of incoming disasters. It was at that point an almost completely defenseless setting: large portions of its police force had deserted, many of its neighborhoods were underwater, and an almost endless array of easily raided shops, full of goods, were unoccupied. The *New York Times* informed its readers the day after Katrina: "These are not individuals looting. They are large groups of armed individuals."[38] And then, a day later: "Chaos gripped New Orleans...as looters ran wild...brazenly ripped open gates and ransacked stores for food, clothing, television sets, computers, jewelry, and guns."[39] And guns! The plot thickens. The *Washington Post* offered: "Even as the floodwaters rose, looters roamed the city, ransacking department stores and grocery stores and floating their spoils away in plastic bags...by nightfall, the pillage was

FIGURE 2.4. Hastily scrawled notices that "looters will be shot" were left in many places around New Orleans, including this shop window on St. Charles Avenue. Photo © Charlie Varley/varleypix.com, 2005.

widespread."[40] The Associated Press reported that "officials watched help-lessly as looters around the city ransacked stores for food, clothing, ap-pliances, and guns."[41] The article quoted a highly respected New Orleans councilwoman: "The looting is out of control. The French Quarter has been attacked."

On Wednesday, August 31, Louisiana Governor Kathleen Blanco had heard enough. She ordered local police and the National Guard to suspend their rescue efforts and concentrate on restoring public order. She warned about the coming of National Guard units: "These troops are fresh back from Iraq, well-trained, experienced, battle-tested.... They have M16s and they're locked and loaded. These troops know how to shoot and kill, and they are more than willing to do so if necessary. And I expect they will."[42] It was clear from that moment forward that the needs of a suffering people would be set aside to protect property and enforce the customary level of civility counted on by the already comfortable. Ray Nagin, the mayor of New Orleans, followed the same line of reasoning when he ordered most of his remaining police officers to set aside their search-and-rescue mis-sion and concentrate on orderliness in the streets.

Those reactions to what most observers understand as "looting" were so far off the scale that they simply belonged to a different category of social event, a different species of human hysteria and dread. And that conclusion requires us to turn to a new line of inquiry: Who was behav-ing on the streets of the city in the manner that Blanco and Nagin and so many others assumed to be the case? What reason would there have been for such behavior?

There is no question that some people were taking advantage of the fluid situation and stealing valuables for future use. Some did so in full view of television cameras, and those cameras were also at work when the most brazen of all looters, police officers in full uniform, took off with the same spoils. That activity was "larceny" by any standard, but it was not treated that way by authorities later.

At the same time, New Orleans was full of people in desperate need of water, food, and other necessities to keep their families as well as them-selves alive. The sociologist Kathleen Tierney once described their efforts as "acquiring the means of subsistence." And a young African American man met by one of us on the streets of New Orleans not long after Katrina said largely the same thing, with a warm and mischievous smile: "Man, we was just living off the land." That is exactly what country people from other parts of Louisiana do in difficult times, and what most of the rest of us would do in the same circumstances.

The most widely "looted" items, according to one accounting, were disposable diapers, dry shoes, clothing, foods of all kinds, and medications.[43] Not guns. Not jewelry. Not television sets. "To meet basic needs" is surely the best answer to the question of why people did what they did.

The answer to the question of who it was doing the "looting" takes a moment as well. It is probably reasonable to say that every African American for miles around knew where the line was drawn between "requisitioning" and what the authorities called "looting," between "stealing" and "commandeering." Kanye West, an often outspoken rapper, said of the media during a live television broadcast: "If you see a Black family, it says they're looting. If you see a White family, it says they're looking for food."[44] A church deacon named Harold Toussaint said in an interview: "Yeah, it was interesting. If you were White, you were commandeering a boat. If you were Black, you were stealing it. If you were White, you were providing for your family. If you were Black, you were looting."[45] Any number of others spoke of that dividing line in the same way as Toussaint (from whom we will hear again later). It was clearly a color line. Gary Rivlin retells a story that made the rounds at the time:

> Van Jones, an environmentalist and civil rights activist, juxtaposed a pair of wire-service photos he had found online. The caption on one picturing a young White couple: "Two residents wade through chest-deep water after finding bread and soda from a local grocery store after Hurricane Katrina came through the area." The caption accompanying a photo of an African American: "A young man walks through chest-high floodwater after looting a grocery store in New Orleans on Tuesday, August 30, 2005." Apparently, "Black people 'loot' food," Jones concluded, while "Whites 'find' food."[46]

It is also worth noting that the White man and woman mentioned above were assumed to be "residents" while the young Black man was not. He was simply labeled a "looter," a term suggesting that he came from somewhere else and did not belong there.[47]

It was not long before newscasters reached even deeper into the realms of darkness and terror to tell a story of insiders and outsiders as they viewed the urban scene surrounding them. What they thought they saw was a level of disorder and criminality they had never witnessed before—at least not within the borders of their own homeland. Most of us have only fading memories of New Orleans in the days following Katrina, but many will remember that the early news stories from that devastated location were almost unanimous in reporting that something truly depraved—something degenerate, sinister, menacing—was taking place there. Police officers and rescue vehicles were being fired upon by residents of the city. Armed bands were ready to take over the business district and the homes of the rich. Anarchy was loose in the land. Homeowners in undamaged parts of the city sat on their front porches, rifles across their knees, explaining to reporters from out of town what to them was a simple and obvious fact: they were about to be attacked. How? "Under cover of darkness." And by whom? "Well, you know. Them."

Maureen Dowd of the *New York Times* described New Orleans as "a snake pit of anarchy, death, looting, raping, marauding thugs."[48] The *London Financial Times* seemed to be so excited that it simply abandoned the usual rules of grammar, describing the Convention Center as a place where "girls and boys were raped in the dark and had their throats cut and bodies were stuffed in the kitchens while looters and madmen exchanged fire with weapons they had looted."[49] A Fox News correspondent lamented: "There are so many murders taking place. There are rapes, other violent crimes taking place in New Orleans."[50]

The two city officials in the best position to provide a mature perspective on all that excitement were participating in the mania. Mayor Nagin appeared on *The Oprah Winfrey Show* and declared that the people of New Orleans—his fellow townspeople, after all, the people who had elected him mayor—had reverted to "an almost animalistic state" as a consequence of witnessing the mayhem surrounding them: "Watching hooligans killing people, raping people." Eddie Compass, the New Orleans chief of police, added that the Superdome had become a place where "little babies" were "getting raped," and in another live interview he said that "armed crowds" were "shooting at rescue personnel."[51]

Dan Baum remembers that "lurid rumors" swept across his city then. "A creepy compulsion to believe the worst distorted what New Orleans saw, heard, and felt."[52] The same can be said of most of the newscasters who had come to town to cast a cool, sober eye on what was happening there. What they conveyed to their audiences was a scene of human depravity and outright terror that went beyond any reasonable level of imagining. ABC reported that "four days after the hurricane hit, New Orleans was still plagued by gun battles and rapes, with gangs of looters and carjackers roving the streets as bodies were left lying by the roadside."[53] *Time* magazine published the news that "snipers fired at ambulances, and invading looters demanded that doctors turn over whatever drugs they had. Hijackers shot the tires of fleeing vehicles."[54]

In a Fox News television broadcast, a correspondent suggested—with accompanying footage on the screen—that New Orleans "looks like the Wild West. We've got guys riding around in pick-ups with semi-automatics." He did not seem to know or care to elaborate that these "guys" were very likely members of private security teams hired by the wealthy to protect their property. He went on to say, without further comment, that fires could be seen burning in the distance. A fellow reporter back in the New York studio guessed that the fire was likely set "for no reason but just the joy of arson....Clearly it's a sick joy." A *Los Angeles Times* report described the city's "rapid decline into chaos" with a scattered list of atrocities:

> Snipers threatened hospital evacuations and a mass bus caravan....Corpses were found outside the city's decaying Convention Center...weakened refugees collapsed amid enraged crowds....At nightfall, heavily armed police and National Guard troops took positions on rooftops, scanning for snipers and armed mobs as seething crowds of refugees milled below, desperate to flee. Gunfire crackled in the distance....[There was] an increasing number of rapes and beatings....New Orleans police were overwhelmed and in some instances outgunned by snipers who holed up in abandoned buildings and store fronts....An unseen sniper, holed up in a nearby window, fired sporadically at soldiers and pedestrians.[55]

A CNN program two days after Katrina spoke of "very discouraging reports out of New Orleans tonight about bands of rapists going from block to block, people walking around on feces, dead bodies floating everywhere. And we know that sniper fire continues....We are getting reports that describe it as a nightmare of crime, human waste, rotten food, dead bodies."[56] The *Miami Herald* reported that a "major city was all but disintegrated....Bodies floated down streets. Defeated survivors waded waist-deep and ghost-like through floods. Packs of looters rampaged through the ruins and armed themselves with stolen weapons, and gunfire echoed through the city."[57] The *New York Daily News* joined that growing consensus with fervor: "Corpses littered the sodden streets. Snipers fired on cops and rescue workers. Gangs of looters took anything that was not nailed down."[58] The Associated Press, to bring this recital to a close, declared that New Orleans had "descended into anarchy" as "corpses lay abandoned in street medians, fights broke out...a menacing landscape of disorder and fear."[59] And to add to the distress, sharks from Lake Pontchartrain were reportedly observed swimming in the waters of the Business District. Sharks!

If that rapid string of grisly reports reminds one a bit of machine-gun fire—*crack-crack-crack-crack*—it might indeed be the right image to keep in mind. It is easy to suppose that it felt like that to news gatherers as the reports poured in, and it is easy to suppose that it felt like that to producers trying to organize them into a coherent account. Citizens of the city of New Orleans had been accused by then of a remarkable array of crimes, misdemeanors, and other evils: looting, grand larceny, murder, child rape, sodomy, insurrection, treason, and even, in one sad report, cannibalism.

A PAUSE TO RECONSIDER

There was good news on its way, even if it was a long time in coming: virtually none of those wild and malicious reports turned out to be true. There were no bullet holes in rescue vehicles. Almost all of those gruesome tales of rapes and murders and other dark atrocities were figments of the surreal, macabre imagination that governed the mood of New Orleans. Three weeks after Katrina had made its appearance on the mainland, the media recovered from its frenzy and began to wonder about its own veracity. It was a time of reconsideration, reflection, and even repentance.

The first voice to be heard in what would soon become a resounding chorus was very likely to have been David Carr of the *New York Times*, who deserves a place in the annals of responsible journalism. In a story entitled "More Horrible Than Truth" and dated September 19, 2005, he wrote:

> Disaster has a way of bringing out the best and the worst instincts in the news media. It is a grand thing that during the most terrible days of Hurricane Katrina, many reporters found their gag reflex and stopped swallowing pat excuses from public officials. But the media's willingness to report thinly attributed rumors may have also contributed to a kind of cultural wreckage that will not clean up easily.... Many instances of the lurid libretto of widespread disorder... that filled the airwaves and newspapers have yet to be established or proved, as far as anyone can determine. And many of the urban legends that sprang up—the systematic rape of children, the slitting of a 7-year-old's throat—so far seem to be exactly that.[60]

A flurry of similar reconsiderations and acknowledgments of error soon followed throughout the countryside. Donna Britt in the *Washington Post*: "In Katrina's Wake, Inaccurate Rumors Sullied Victims." Susanna

Rosenblatt of the *Los Angeles Times*: "Katrina Takes a Toll on Truth, News Accuracy." Jim Dwyer and Christopher Drew of the *New York Times*, three days after the David Carr piece: "Fear Exceeded Crime's Reality in New Orleans."

A report that appeared not long after this period of reconsideration and retraction was offered by Brian Thevenot, a reporter for the *Times-Picayune*. He told his readers of the time he walked into the Convention Center through the food service entrance a few days after the flood and encountered what he thought to be "four stinking, decomposing corpses."[61] He considered pulling back the sheets to take a look, as any reporter might, but chose not to. A moment later, he was informed by two National Guard soldiers in charge that "30 or 40" bodies were stored in the freezer. He did not take a look there either. "Too gruesome," he remembered thinking later. So he took the word of those two soldiers as established information, including the report that one of those bodies was a "7-year-old girl with her throat cut," and passed on that grim inventory as authentic in a newspaper account a week after Katrina. When the freezer was opened soon afterward, not a trace was to be found of any corpses. It turned out that the two soldiers had not investigated either—too gruesome?—and had accepted the information as fact from yet someone else. Whatever the soldiers' responsibility, that was poor journalism on Thevenot's part by any professional standard, as he clearly stated:

> I retell this story...as an example of how one of hundreds of myths got reported in the early days of Katrina's aftermath. A colleague and I corrected the freezer report—along with a slew of other rumors and myths transmitted by the media.... In that piece we sought to separate fact from fiction on the issue of reported violence in the Superdome and Convention Center. We hadn't anticipated the massive shockwave of self-correction. [It was] a moment of mass-scale media introspection that ultimately resulted in a healthy revision of history's first draft.[62]

A lengthy segment of the *PBS NewsHour* that aired on September 29, 2005, dealt with the coverage of Katrina in some detail.[63] A broadcast like that consists of images on the screen for the eye to look at and voices for the ear to listen to, and we can only offer the latter here, where we draw heavily on the transcript from that segment.

Jeffrey Brown, the moderator, asserted at one point, "There was also intense focus on alleged violence and mayhem within the city," whereupon we hear the voice of a reporter: "All kinds of reports of looting, fires, violence—thugs shooting at rescue crews." After Brown says, "Reporters talked to people who said they were witnesses to atrocities inside the Superdome and the Convention Center," we hear another reporter's voice: "You got these young teenage boys running around up here raping those girls." Brown: "But in recent days, many of those accounts have been called into question. While there was violence and great suffering in the city, it now appears that many of the most alarming reports may have been the product of rumor rather than known fact."

Next is the voice of Col. Jacques Thibodeaux of the Louisiana National Guard: "I've heard of situations and rumors of rapes and murders and complete lawlessness in both the Superdome and the Convention Center. And I can tell you that I was in both those locations, and those are just false. Those things didn't happen."

Three reporters then gather around a small conference table with Jeffrey Brown for a broader conversation. One of them suggests that "I think I can be forgiven in this case for believing a police chief when he says something under those circumstances, or for believing a mayor when he says something under those circumstances." But another reporter, Hugh Hewitt, is withering in his contempt for his colleagues in general:

> In fact, they were reporting lies.... American media threw everything they had at this story, all the bureaus, all the networks, everything went to New Orleans, and yet they could not find a way to get inside the Convention Center, they could not find a way to get inside the Superdome to dispel the lurid, the hysterical, the salaciousness of the reporting. I have especially in mind the throat-slashed 7-year-old girl who had been gang-raped at the Convention Center. Didn't happen. In fact, there were no rapes at the Convention Center or the Superdome that have been corroborated in any way. But America was riveted by this reporting. It was a wholesale collapse of the media's own levees.... I think it led to one of the worst weeks of reporting in the history of American media.... I think some of the journalists involved—particularly the anchors—became so caught up in their own persona and their own celebrity that they missed important and obvious stories.

Most of those reporters that Hewitt was referring to, of course, had rarely if ever been near the places they were describing so vividly. They were relying on information from local persons who were themselves caught up in the frenzy and who passed on those reports of slayings and other unspeakable atrocities. Looking back, it is clear that those informants never claimed to have *witnessed* the horrors they were speaking of. They just *knew* that those things had taken place. They *sensed* them, perhaps. One can conclude, then, that the newscasters were relying on what turned out to be the least reliable informants to be found in the vicinity. And perhaps even more to the point, they were listening to and depending on the very individuals who ought to have been their prime subject matter and the objects of their most intensive investigative reporting. The fears and uncertainties that had driven those informants to such dire conclusions were a major contributor to the furor that the newspersons had come to town to understand and report on. In a very real sense, not only were their fears a critical part of the news, but in fact *they were* the news, and not just reporters of it.

The Superdome had become a refuge for tens of thousands of persons, and Chief of Police Compass had described it as a battlefield littered with corpses. He expected to find at least two hundred of them and arranged for refrigerator trucks to be brought up to the front entrance to cart them away when the site was finally evacuated. The actual roster turned out to be six bodies. Four had died of what the coroner called "natural causes," almost surely meaning that death had come from old age and frailty. One died of an overdose. One committed suicide.

Similarly, at the Convention Center—the location where those "little babies" were so threatened, according to Compass—the same expectations prevailed and the same refrigerator trucks were drawn up to the front door. The body count there was four: three people, again, had died "naturally," and one had suffered a "puncture wound" in an *actual* homicide. Estimates suggest that perhaps as many as fifty thousand people had sought refuge at those two shelters, but under the most desperate circumstances imaginable, only one had expired at the hand of another. Official reports rarely provide full information in situations like these, but this might well have been the lowest homicide rate recorded over a four-day period in that part of New Orleans in modern times.

Most newspapers that had contributed to the racist hysteria about conditions in the Superdome and Convention Center—the *New York Times*, the *Washington Post*, the *Los Angeles Times*, and, as just noted, the hometown *Times-Picayune*—went out of their way to acknowledge the many inaccuracies and downright falsehoods they had managed to spread. Chief Compass, to his great credit, not only admitted that many of his reports had turned out to be inaccurate, but then added: "We have no official reports that document any murder. Not one official report of rape or sexual assault." The New Orleans police lieutenant who headed the department's sex crimes unit said that he and his officers were inside the Superdome "and ran down every rumor of rape or atrocity." They made two arrests for attempted sexual attack, but in the end concluded that the other attacks "did not happen."[64]

UNDERSTANDING THE COSTS

After the media recovered from "the collapse of its own levees," as Hugh Hewitt had called it, it went about its tasks more rationally. But as a long-term consequence of that grotesque misreading of what was taking place on the streets of New Orleans, rescue efforts were stalled at all levels, and in that long pause people suffered, died, and lost any belief they may have harbored that they could depend on the goodwill of their city, their state, and their country. The cost in human life and human dignity was tremendous and lasts to this day.

A number of people from President Bush down to everyday reporters were roundly criticized for referring to residents of the affected areas who were being driven out of their homes as "refugees," which is usually taken to mean "aliens," "outsiders," or "foreigners." Whether Bush or any of the others had that definition in mind, consciously or unconsciously, we can only guess. But local survivors were known to employ that same term to describe their own status, a usage that would be fully approved by *Merriam-Webster's Dictionary*, which defines "refugee" as "a person who flees to a foreign country or power" to escape danger or persecution." The dictionary's qualifier, "to a foreign country or power," helps explain some of the confusion and righteous anger that emanated from different corners. Rev. Jesse Jackson, for his part, reminded the news media that the people of New Orleans were "*citizens* displaced by a disaster." We are doing a lot of playing with words here, but a good case can be made that a considerable number of Black Americans accepted the treatment of Black residents of New Orleans at the hands of the media and their own government as further evidence of something they had long suspected—that they really were outsiders and that their lives mattered less.

The outside world had been informed in no uncertain terms that New Orleans was in the midst of an organized insurgency, and that murder, rape, and every imaginable form of violence ruled the city streets. It seemed obvious in such circumstances that humanitarian aid had to be postponed, if not set aside altogether. In effect, the reigning emergency was made out to be, *not* that people were going without water or food or shelter, but that disorder ruled, innocents were being assaulted, guns were being stolen, and—no small matter to the business elite—private property was being jeopardized.

The suspension of aid led to long delays in the provision of medical care, the restoration of critical infrastructure, and the delivery of essential water and food, sanitary supplies, and life-sustaining medications of many kinds. Kathleen Tierney and Christine A. Bevc put it bluntly:

> Within three days after Katrina made landfall, the governor of Louisiana and the mayor of New Orleans suspended lifesaving operations in New Orleans and ordered emergency responders to concentrate on arresting looters and deterring crime instead—an order that may have amounted to a death sentence for stranded victims in desperate need of rescue.[65]

Local incidents that reflected this sudden shift in focus could be found all over New Orleans and its surrounding areas. Some of them verge on the ridiculous in the retelling, but at the time the tension in the air was formidable. In one instance, paramedics were delayed for a full ten hours before being able to respond to a medical emergency in Slidell, then reachable only by boat, because of a state trooper's report that a mob of armed people had taken over all the available vessels. Not so. In another instance, a company put its fleet of working ambulances under lock and key upon hearing a report that a nearby firehouse had been looted by armed thugs. Once again, not so. When a deputy sheriff from St. Bernard Parish radioed for help because he was under attack by a sniper, a fully armed police SWAT team accompanied by National Guard troops stormed into the neighborhood, only to discover that the sniper fire came from "the relief valve of a gas tank that popped open every few minutes."[66]

Perhaps startled by that story of sniper fire, residents and law enforcement personnel in St. Bernard Parish worked together to stack flooded cars and trucks across St. Bernard Highway. Whatever the motivation, their purpose was clear. They were attempting to create a barricade on the main thoroughfare between the overwhelmingly White St. Bernard Parish and the majority-Black Orleans Parish neighborhood to the north.

And so it went throughout the city. Truck drivers charged with bringing badly needed supplies into the city, upon hearing the frightful reports issuing from New Orleans, pulled over to the side of the road and refused to continue. There they were in a good position to notice the departure of a host of police officers who apparently had concluded that remaining in

FIGURE 2.5. Vehicles stacked to impede movement into St. Bernard Parish.
Photo © William Freudenburg, 2005.

their assigned posts in the city was well beyond the call of duty. The flow of essential resources into New Orleans was essentially paralyzed.

We have no way of learning how many people simply slumped over and died in spirit as well as in body as a result of the decision by authorities to view the restoration of order and the protection of private property as higher priorities than rescuing the desperate, and we have no way of assessing how many people spent the rest of their lives suffering from avoidable physical and emotional injuries. Those will have to remain unaccounted costs in this sad audit.

One additional cost is worth mentioning before we turn to other concerns. The people of New Orleans were deeply insulted by their portrayal to fellow citizens of their own land and others throughout the rest of the world as living on the edge of insurrection, as people fully capable of murdering and raping their neighbors under cover of darkness. One observer thought that the local people were being "cheated" by that account, and another accused the media of "broadly stigmatizing a city and its people."[67] It was, in the view of many, a source of deep humiliation. A betrayal even.

Military assistance, too, was delayed for quite some time by what everyone assumed to be the lawlessness that reigned in New Orleans. But before long, about seventy thousand troops made their way into the city: roughly two-thirds were members of the National Guard, and one-third were active-duty soldiers in divisions like the 82nd Airborne and the 1st Cavalry. In addition, a large number of uniformed, heavily armed persons from private security contractors like Blackwater USA and ArmorCorps entered the area; some were employed by federal agencies, and others were on contract with local businesses or well-to-do property owners.

The main intelligence available to those troops, of course, came from the news media, so what they were about to encounter was assumed to be a violent concentration of people who had slain and raped and maimed neighbors in the thousands, in addition to plundering everything in sight. They may have assumed that these folks were now planning an outright rebellion. The troops preparing to enter that inferno, trained in facing fierce enemy strongholds on the battlefields of Iraq and Afghanistan and elsewhere, were steeled to make sure that they would not be outgunned either in arms or in sheer ferocity. They had been invited, in some cases even encouraged, to fire on their fellow citizens. The *Army Times* announced on September 2, four days after the first appearance of the flood, that "combat operations were now underway on the streets.... This place is going to look like Little Somalia.... This will be a combat operation to get this city back under control."[68] ABC News spoke to a National Guard member who "voiced little hesitation at using deadly force—a skill honed in Iraq—on the streets of New Orleans. 'If we're out in the streets, we'll fight back and shoot until we kill them.'" The report continued: "Just the smell and feel of a war zone in the city put soldiers on edge." The same source reported that New Orleans was a field of open combat where a National Guardsman had been shot outside the Superdome and guns had been fired "at a Chinook helicopter" while it took part in an effort to evacuate "refugees" from the stadium.

It is probably fair to say, then, that those entering troops often increased the local tension and made an already difficult situation worse. Deacon Harold Toussaint, whom we quoted earlier, offered the following account in an interview with the legal scholar D'Ann Penner:

> One afternoon I was on the bridge in front of the building by City Park on Bayou St. John and Esplanade, and we saw the federal troops pass by in some kind of black uniforms [that] said FEDERAL POLICE on the

back. There were three or four of them in a bulldozer. A lone National Guardsman from the building [I was in front of]...said to me, "Harold, go tell the Federal Police that they need to come over here with a bulldozer because we might have to knock down some posts or something else to make room for a helicopter landing." I had on a short-sleeved shirt and my pants were wet. I had no place to hide a weapon. As I approached them, I just waved my hand out and said, "the guardsman over there; he needs to talk to you." The Federal Police pointed their M16s at me and said, "Get back! Get back! Get back!" I raised both of my hands up and said "No, I'm trying to tell you that the Guardsman says he needs your help." Again, "Get back! Get back! Get back!"

I felt they were ready to shoot me. They wouldn't let me get within 10 yards of them. What if someone was dying and needed their help? I felt that [what was happening] right there explained what was happening elsewhere in the city. These people see us as enemy combatants. They're not here *for* us. All that these federal troops could see was that I was Black, and Blacks are criminals. That's what I got from them when we needed them most. It was very discouraging to be treated as an enemy combatant rather than someone who needed to be rescued.[69]

Judging from the description of their uniforms, those "Federal Police" were probably civilians in the employ of Blackwater rather than National Guardsmen, but whether knowing that would have made a difference to Toussaint is unlikely. They were agents of a government whose responsibility was to care for its people. Dan Baum reported: "Adding to the Dodge City atmosphere were such private soldiers as those of Blackwater, who lurked on the broad steps of many mansions, draped in automatic weapons. As I sat on the porch of a house on tranquil St. Charles Avenue on Saturday night after the storm, a red color dot from a gunsight moved slowly across my chest."[70] That would not have been very likely to reduce the feelings of apprehension that pervaded the atmosphere of the city.

The *Los Angeles Times* reported that the incoming troops "took positions on rooftops, scanning for snipers and armed mobs as seething crowds of refugees milled below, desperate to flee. Gunfire cracked in the distance."[71] The *Washington Post* offered an article subtitled "It's Like Baghdad on a Bad Day."[72] It was "a lawless, deadly war zone," CNN said of the disaster-affected area where troops were being deployed. Yet another report likened "the events in New Orleans" to "the urban insurgency the US military currently faces in Iraq."[73]

FIGURE 2.6. A father pleads for help and holds his child above his head while trying to capture the attention of Louisiana National Guard members. Photo © Charlie Varley/varleypix.com, 2005.

But after a short while it became obvious that there were no armed insurgents lurking in the shadows or snipers hidden in dark upper stories. Not one soldier had been wounded by enemy fire. Troops geared for outright combat came to recognize that they were encountering a scene of human confusion and pain rather than one of fierce hostility. Parents pleaded with soldiers, "Take my baby, my baby, take my baby first!" as they tried to find a way out of the city. It was not long before those in charge became a source of rationality. They were drawing on a perspective shaped by actual experience rather than one shaped by the panic of officials and others.[74] They were witnessing a humanitarian crisis unfolding.

Soon enough, a relative calm began to settle over the city. This shift in temper became crystal clear when what the city regarded as its prominent "snake pits" of anarchy and chaos, the Superdome and the Convention Center, were visited by federal troops ready for warfare. Reporters for the *Times-Picayune* summarized what took place then:

> Rumors of rampant violence at the Convention Center prompted Louisiana National Guard Lt. Col. Jacques Thibodeaux [to] put together a 1,000-man force of soldiers and police in full battle gear to secure the center September 2nd at about noon. It took only 20 minutes to take control, and soldiers met no resistance, Thibodeaux said. What the soldiers found—elderly people and infants near death without food, water, and medicine; crowds living in filth—shocked them more than anything they'd seen in combat zones overseas. But they found no evidence, witnesses, or victims of any killings, rapes, or beatings, Thibodeaux said. Another commander who was soon to arrive, Lt. Col. John Edwards of the Arkansas National Guard, said the crowd welcomed the soldiers. "It reminded me of the liberation of France in World War II. There were people cheering; one boy even saluted," he said. "We never—never once—encountered any hostility."[75]

The modern version of the 1815 Battle of New Orleans was over. It had never really begun.

UNDER COVER OF DARKNESS

As we round out this discussion of what happened on the streets of New Orleans, we will briefly, and very cautiously, venture into murky conceptual terrain to consider what kinds of thought processing might have been at work on those unsettled streets and in those unsettled minds. A good part of the testimony sent out into the world about what was happening in New Orleans came from persons who lived there describing events that seemed to have taken place, in a common expression at the time, "under cover of darkness." That could mean "nighttime," when vision was uncertain, or it could mean "hidden from sight." In either case, however, the phrase referred to "things we know to have happened" even though no one appears to have witnessed them directly. That kind of testimony puts us in murky terrain, to be sure, but it is important to enter it in order to understand those times. Mayor Nagin, trying to rest in a hotel room, was sure that he heard gunshots outside on the streets below. He later wrote: "I really did not think we'd make it through Wednesday night without an Armageddon-like war occurring in the total darkness."[76]

Fox News reported that "violent gangs are roaming the streets at night, hidden by cover of darkness."[77] NBC spoke of persons in deep fear "hiding from people they can't even see." The *New York Times* described a period of time when "violence raged inside the Convention Center" and "police SWAT team members found themselves plunging into the darkness, guided by the muzzle flashes of thugs' handguns."[78] Whoever the *Times* was relying on as a source at that point saw "flashes" of something out there in the darkness and assumed that the use of firearms was responsible for them—a remarkable leap from observation to conclusion, especially when one takes into account that no one in that densely crowded space, SWAT team member or anyone else, was hit by one of those bullets. By every professional standard one can draw on, coming to such a conclusion simply did not qualify as reasonable reportage. And those conclusions had consequences. Later the *Times* proposed that "terror from crimes seen and unseen, real and rumored, played a key role in slowing down troop deployments to New Orleans as well as medical evacuations."[79]

We all "saw" amazing images, if only in our mind's eye, of what was taking place on the streets of New Orleans right after Katrina. But the most searing of those pictures were formed almost entirely by words rather than by anything visual. Reports of chaos, violence, and depravity were the work of reporters looking for sensational happenings and of public officials looking for words that could express the horror they sensed in the world around them. But there were no photos or videos of anything that even came close to a killing, a roving gang, a sniper at work, machine guns in civilian hands, or anything of the sort. If we seek physical evidence of those terrors, there is little to be found, if any at all. The information that reporters were depending on came in large part from persons who *sensed* it, *felt* it, perhaps even *heard* it in the shadows of the day and in the echoes and uneasy silences of the night. W. Joseph Campbell, in a volume entitled *Getting It Wrong: Ten of the Greatest Misreported Stories in American Journalism*, writes:

> Major Ed Bush of the Louisiana National Guard, who was stationed at the Superdome during the most wretched days after the hurricane struck, offered a sense of how the feedback loop caused confusion, consternation, and fresh rumors. "People would hear something on the radio and come [to me] and say that people were getting raped in the bathroom or someone had been murdered," Bush told the *Washington Post*. "I would say, 'Ma'am, where?' I would tell them if there were bodies, my guys would find them. Everybody heard, nobody saw."

And that raises yet another question as we make our way carefully through this terrain: What does it mean to *see* something? It means to observe it with one's own eyes, in one sense, but it also means to be satisfied that it actually happened. It is not always what the eyes behold that matters in the long term, but what the brain registers and the imagination makes of it. When people say, "I see your point," or, "I see what you mean," they are not speaking of vision in the physical sense of the term.

A colleague of ours, Jessica Pardee, brought that matter up in her study focusing on the experiences of low-income African American women who had survived the disaster and its aftereffects. Her sample included several women who spent time in the Superdome or the Convention Center and were sure that they had seen horrifying events taking place there. These were "the deep traumas" that women "did confirm during their time stranded in those shelters of last resort," as Pardee described it.[80] One of her interviewees said:

> They attacking, raping, killing, raping the children. People jumping off the Superdome, killing themselves; killing the guards.... Some man on top of the roof, he was trying to get through to where the buses were going out, he shooting...so the National Guard shot him in the head. He fell into the water. There was shooting all over the place. We had to get down because snipers set on trying to shoot us.[81]

Another one of Pardee's interviewees told her that

> there was rapes and killings. A baby was raped, and it was right down from us—the baby was raped and killed, and then set on a pile of trash. A

15-year-old girl was raped.... The man had his throat slashed from ear to ear.... There was one whole family who got killed.... One of the guards got shot. It was horrible in there. *You had to be there to see it.* They had gangs and homosexuals and drugs.... It was like animals in there.[82]

In his *New York Times* article "Superdome: Haven Quickly Becomes an Ordeal," Joseph B. Treaster wrote of a young resident who "stammered hysterically as she recounted seeing two young girls being raped in one of the women's bathrooms. 'A lot of people saw it, but they were afraid to do anything,' she said. 'He ran past all of us.'"[83] "Saw it" in this context almost surely means "knew of it." And in most of that kind of testimony, if you look carefully, it becomes more and more likely that few of those respondents are speaking of horrors they had witnessed with their own eyes. They were aware of them, had heard about them, perhaps even could feel them in the tense terror of their surroundings.

There are reality tests available too, particularly in the case of the Superdome and Convention Center. When the time came to survey the endless debris spread about after the shelter was emptied of people, a different category of "fact" was brought to bear.[84] One of these facts is that there were no corpses in that wreckage. We can be absolutely sure that a man with his throat slashed from ear to ear, a murdered baby left on a pile of debris, a whole family slain, were creations of the mind—ones that were widely repeated under those terrifying and inhumane circumstances, but creations nonetheless. As for the other dark memories, the available data cannot offer this level of certainty, but there are tests of probability as well. We do not want to be too macabre here, but the number of infant rapes rumored and reported at the height of the furor was not supported by verifiable medical evidence either. An epidemic of infant rape does not fit into the realm of the probable.

One observer, trying to find the right words to convey what he was experiencing, said: "Imagine your worst nightmare and multiply that times 100." Suppose that we were to take that suggestion: instead of recording what people remembered seeing out there in the raw darkness, we would ask them, "What is the worst thing you can imagine?" The worst sin. The worst immorality. The worst villainy. That question is almost an invitation to *see* that horror in the mind's eye and to give it shape, give it a name, find words to convey it. And when people sense that horror in the blurry landscape around them—hear it maybe, or even smell it—they *know* what it is and can tell others what they have sensed. We can envision people saying things such as, "The worst thing I can imagine is a big, menacing man closing in on a helpless infant." Or "The worst thing I can imagine is a pack of armed men with red eyes aflame in the dark and looking for...." It is important to remember as we ponder such matters that we are speaking of disaster survivors and emergency responders who experienced levels of tension and disorientation that most of us will never fully know.

The problems posed by remarks recorded in the available data on things that happened "under cover of darkness" are matched in some ways by those employing the pronouns "them" and "they." As we related earlier, homeowners in undamaged areas surrounding New Orleans were interviewed in the days following Katrina as they sat on their front porches. They explained to reporters from out of town what to them were simple and obvious facts. Many of those exchanges went something like this:

"We are about to be attacked."

"How?"

"Under cover of darkness."

"By whom?

"Well, you know, *them.*"

You will be learning later in this chapter about a time when a large group of desperate people tried to make their way across a bridge separating the flooded city of New Orleans from a dry suburb on the other side of the Mississippi River. The crowd was stopped in its tracks by police officers armed with assault rifles, some of whom fired into the air for emphasis. One resident of the suburb described herself as "ecstatic" about the barricading of the bridge, noting that "*they* were looting, and *they* were shooting, and we didn't want that over here."[85] No one thought it necessary to ask the White suburbanite who "they" were.

Dan Baum heard a similarly ugly remark from a local merchant who said, .38 pistol in hand, "If you let them get started, there's no telling where it will end."[86] *Them.* Another came from a police sergeant: "If I were you, I'd get the hell out of here. Tonight they're going to waste Whites, and they don't care which ones."[87] *They.*

And even without those telltale pronouns "them" and "they," it is quite clear who the speakers have in mind in comments like the following. A New Orleans police sergeant, coming upon a scene of suspected looting, suggested: "The nation's realizing what kind of criminals we have here." New Orleans Homeland Security representative Terry Ebbert, "startled by the sheer mass of looting," declared that those "cockroaches need to be dealt with." And another observer said: "As far as the gunfire, yeah, it was there, and some of it was directed at law enforcement and some of it was directed at emergency workers. Which goes to show you the mentality of the element you are dealing with." A townsperson said: "You just know what those outlaws are up to. You can see it in their eyes." The speaker of that line, we can be sure, never really looked into those outlaws' eyes. He was inadvertently speaking about what his own eyes saw when he came across someone with skin darker than his own.

Three years later, the widely discredited media personality Rush Limbaugh compared a flood in Cedar Rapids, Iowa, to the one that had taken place in 2005 in New Orleans. In Cedar Rapids, he noted, "I see people working together," and he then added:

> I see people trying to save their property. I don't see a bunch of people running around, waving guns at helicopters. I don't see people running, shooting at cops. I don't see a bunch of people raping people on the street. I don't see a bunch of people...whining and moaning—Where's FEMA? Where's Bush? I see the heartland of America. When I see Iowa, I see the backbone of America.[88]

The racial categories White and Black do not appear anywhere in that inane outburst, but they are there, literally with a vengeance. It is a reasonable guess that is exactly what Limbaugh intended his audience to see. Any news host who did not understand, years after the fact, what the rest of his colleagues acknowledged to have been a humiliating failure of their craft had simply shifted into a very different category of theater.

In many respects, the word "darkness" in the phrase "under cover of darkness" has as much to do with race as it does with the time of day or with things hidden out of sight. One is tempted to say—because it seems so obvious—that "it goes without saying" that the comments cited here that contain the pronoun "them" are referring to, or hinting at, African Americans. But it *did* go without saying in most of those news reports, and that makes it all the more important that it not go without saying in later discussions of what happened on the streets of New Orleans after Katrina.[89]

Such reflections lead us to consider what remain, all these years later, the most important questions to emerge from those times. Early media reports about what was happening in New Orleans were not only off the mark, but exceedingly so, incredibly so, and we need to inquire into their origin. Why did so many people in New Orleans believe these reports? Why did the news media, so shrewd and experienced in the ways of the world, believe that they were reporting the truth? And why—no idle inquiry—did so many of us, the listening audience, believe these stories? From what chambers in the heart did our credulousness issue? From what sectors of the social order?

First, the people of the city. One does not need to reach too far back into the historical past or too deeply into the cultural composition of New Orleans to realize that the relationship between Black and White has always been a source of tension and even of menace there.[90] Mitch Landrieu, who ran for mayor five years after Katrina, pledged to "do everything I can...to heal the racial divide that has kept us apart for so long."[91] Nicholas Lehmann, who comes from that part of the world and is a seasoned observer of its ways, wrote in the *New York Review of Books* that the "ancient, ever-present White fear of Black insurrection spiked after Katrina."[92] And Alex de Waal, who wrote a piece entitled "An Imperfect Storm" for the bulletin of the Social Science Research Council, sighed almost audibly in print, noting that "a stricken society fractures along the fault lines that were there all along."[93]

Second, the press. It is only reasonable to suppose that the media were interested in keeping the attention of their audiences fixed intently on "the news." Programmers located in central offices certainly had that object in mind when selecting the items that would be featured in upcoming broadcasts. But the news items pouring into those offices came from reporters out in the field, and there was no question, as they themselves acknowledged afterward, that their attention was drawn to loud horrors far more than to calmer happenings. Public officials, of course, were one source of that kind of news. Under normal circumstances, it would have made sense for reporters to turn to a mayor or a police chief or a governor for information. But these were far from normal circumstances, and those experienced reporters should have realized much sooner that the officials they were relying on were looking at the situation through badly compromised eyes. What does that oversight say about the reporters? It becomes a guessing game once we shift our attention to the media, but among the explanations that we, and they, need to ponder thoughtfully is that the newscasters, too, at some level of consciousness, shared with New Orleans public officials and the people of the city a sense of the capacity for "insurrection" to which Lehmann alluded. W. Joseph Campbell thinks that he saw in their reportage a latent readiness to assume the worst about the "other"—in this case, the poor, mostly Black urban dwellers, with whom affluent mainstream journalists usually have little sustained contact and few shared interests. In the immediate aftermath of the hurricane, reporters engaged in unintentional stereotyping of New Orleans and its poor people and minorities. Thevenot wrote in "Myth-Making in New Orleans" that he had "little doubt that, consciously or unconsciously, some White reporters, and probably a smaller number of Black ones found it more plausible that babies had been raped and children had been knifed in a Black crowd than they would in a theoretical White one."[94]

Indeed, a question raised more than once by persons who have given this subject some serious thought is whether the reports of violence that were said to dominate in the Superdome and the Convention Center would have been anywhere near the same if a majority of those seeking refuge had been White. Jim Amoss of the *Times-Picayune* suggested: "If the Dome and the Convention Center had harbored large numbers of middle-class White people, it would not have been fertile ground for this kind of rumormongering."[95] This statement remains in the realm of the hypothetical because, in reality, White middle-class people rarely access shelters during disasters. Their savings and social networks typically shield them from those settings.

And third, what about the rest of *us*—two letters that signify our nation when capitalized and ourselves when lower-case. Why did so many people living in this country of ours find it so easy to believe what we were hearing from the press during those early reports from the field? One answer has to be that most of us turn to our chosen form of news media as a mostly reliable source of information. Pure and simple. But we also have to ask the same questions of ourselves as we did of the people of New Orleans and members of the press. To what extent does our land as a whole reflect the "racial divide" that Mitch Landrieu referred to when speaking of his New Orleans, the "White fear" that Nicholas Lehmann characterized when speaking of the American South, and the "fault line" that Alex de Waal named when speaking of the country as a whole?

Earlier, we referred to the incident that occurred when a large crowd of desperate people from New Orleans, looking for refuge, tried to pass over a highway bridge that reached across the Mississippi River to the suburb of Gretna. "Small City, Big Heart" was then and is now Gretna's proud motto. The crowd had been told by officials—who may or may not have known what they were talking about—that buses awaited them on the other side of the river to take them to safety. It was a real shock for them to learn that the bridge was blocked by heavily armed police officers who fired rifle shots over their heads. "We're not going to have another Superdome here," they were told loudly. It will come as a surprise to no one if we add that the crowd was largely African American ("them") and that Gretna is predominantly White. Not far from the carefully crafted sign showing the "Big Heart" motto of Gretna one could find a hastily scribbled sign with these words: TRESPASSERS WILL BE SHOT.

The question is this: How well did Gretna's response reflect feelings common to the rest of the land? Nancy Scheper-Hughes, a careful observer of the American cultural landscape, wrote about the Gretna episode in the journal *Anthropology Today* three months after Katrina. She offered an interesting comparison: "Contrast this violent scene with the evacuation of thousands of ordinary people from Lower Manhattan in the wake of 9/11...across a bridge into the safety of Queens. A beautiful historical moment." And so it was. But we also need to ask what would have happened in Lower Manhattan, or any other part of the country, if people coming across that bridge were almost all Black and terrified and pouring into a guarded White neighborhood.

IN THE END

We opened this book by making the case that Katrina was one of the most telling disasters of our times because of what it has suggested about the society we live in and about ourselves. We noted a bit later that reports are still floating up in the mists that continue to obscure meaningful parts of what happened in the time of Katrina.

For instance, a number of slayings and attempted slayings, some of them by police officers and others by local White vigilantes, took place that did not make their way into official records.[96] The *Times-Picayune* reported that city police officers shot eleven persons in the first few days after Katrina.[97] None of the eleven were armed. The police were not all that forthcoming on the subject when asked about it afterwards, in part because the keeping of records was not that high of a priority in those trying days, and in part because keeping the peace seemed to require such things in the world they were imagining then. Little was said about it later. District Attorney Eddie Gordon tried seven officers on murder and attempted murder charges, but they were dismissed for technical reasons by a state court judge. So that process, too, drifted into the mists. Five officers were indicted for civil rights violations at the federal level, and that was the end of that.

An even more somber drama was being played out in Point Algiers, right across the Mississippi from downtown New Orleans, where a group of White vigilantes formed an armed militia not only to protect themselves from attack—that "fear of insurrection" again—but also to keep the streets clear of suspicious people before they could do harm. Eleven persons were known to have been shot in that way, at least two of them fatally, but that number may well have been higher.[98] A local surgeon on the staff of an active trauma center in those days told a reporter from out of town: "We saw a bunch of gunshot wounds. There were a lot of gunshot wounds that went unreported." That same surgeon remembered handling "five or six nonfatal gunshot wounds" as well as three lethal gunshot cases.[99]

It is hard to tell, except in the case of the vigilantes, who was doing the shooting and who was being shot. But based on the available record, it stands entirely to reason that White folks were doing the damage and Black folk were absorbing it.

LOCATING KATRINA

In the years since Katrina, specialists from a number of fields involved in the study of disasters have sought ways to portray the dimensions of that horrifying event. How many people were killed? Where and why did they die? Who suffered physical injury or emotional harm? How much damage was done to human settlements and natural environments? How many people were displaced? And so on.

Accountings of this kind allow us to make comparisons with similar events and even to assign them a rank in the official roster of these events. We can say with some assurance, for example, that Katrina was not the most *lethal* hurricane in recent American history. The Galveston hurricane of 1900, which killed somewhere between 8,000 and 12,000 people, has that dubious distinction.[1] The final death toll for Katrina, although still questionable (for reasons discussed in chapter 3), is typically placed at around 1,800, with the acknowledgment that the final number of dead will never be known.[2] If not the most lethal disaster in US history, Katrina still remains one of the most expensive on record: it generated some $135 billion in insured and uninsured losses.[3]

To do these kinds of calculations, Katrina has to be approached as if it were bounded both in time and in space—as if it took place over a certain stint of time and within a certain stretch of space. One can be very flexible about those boundaries in how the tale is told, but Aristotle's ancient rule of dramatic plots—that they have a beginning, a middle, and an end— applies to historical occurrences as well. Charles Fritz, a true pioneer in the field, offered the following classic definition of "disaster":

> A disaster is an event, concentrated in time and space, in which a
> society or a relatively self-sufficient subdivision of a society under-
> goes severe danger and incurs such losses to its members and physical

appurtenances that the social structure is disrupted and the fulfillment of all or some of essential functions of the society is prevented.[4]

One can introduce qualifications like "the war is never over for the soldier who continues to dream of it at night," or, as we will suggest more than once in this book, "Katrina is a continuing storm for those who still suffer from its effects." For the most part, however, disasters are framed in our memories as interruptions of normalcy that rage for a period of time but are then spoken of in the past tense. We measure that span of time in which disaster occurred by knowing when it began. The disaster now known as Katrina began in the early morning of August 29, 2005. We measure the difference between *then* and *now* when we observe anniversaries and thus give a disaster its place in the flow of history.

In the same way, disasters usually belong to particular locations and are often named for them: in the distant past, the London plague of 1665 and the Lisbon earthquake of 1775; in more recent times, the 2010 Haiti earthquake and the 2011 Joplin tornado. It is hard to know how to speak of disasters without temporal and geographic boundaries of that sort. It is those boundaries that allow us to position them in human experience, even though the damage done may be found throughout a much wider expanse.

This way of framing disasters, however, can be an obstacle to fully understanding them. It contains them in ways that can lead us to seriously underestimate their enduring, and often hidden, effects.

The next two chapters focus on some of the issues posed by locating Katrina *in time* and *in space*. Once again, our emphasis will be largely on New Orleans, not because what happened along the shores of the Gulf and elsewhere does not matter, but because our collective attention turned to the Crescent City as the focal point of Katrina. Thus, in the national experience, New Orleans will remain a source of information about our times and about ourselves.

IN TIME

Historical accounts of Katrina are almost bound to begin with the exact instant the hurricane hit the Gulf Coast. We can narrow that moment down to the minute. But doing so does not tell us anything useful about the origins of the disaster or the mayhem that followed it. The harm done that day and during the days that followed owes a good deal to the winds and the waters that surged up from the coast, but it has far more to do with the way humankind has positioned itself across the surfaces of the land those winds and waters encountered on their charge inland. Virtually everything caught in that path—homes, schools, businesses, roads, bridges, canals—was a human construction. Where, then, should one look for beginnings?

THE LANDSCAPE THAT NATURE MADE

To return to a topic introduced earlier, New Orleans is a seaport in any useful sense of the term. Unlike other seaports located along the East and West Coasts, however, it sits a long way from open seawater—75 miles as the crow flies and double that distance as the Mississippi River makes its leisurely way down to the Gulf. The city lies far away from open water because the entire landscape in between is a rich mixture of water and soil—the gradual buildup of billions of tons of silt that was once topsoil from the heartland of America, now a gift to its southern neighbors.

When the Mississippi flows rapidly, as it tends to do in the northern reaches of its journey, it picks up loose soil particles and carries them along in its momentum. But when the river widens and slows down as it drifts into its southern reaches, it deposits endless layers of that soil along its banks—nature's own levees—and then sends the rest out into what becomes an ever-expanding shoreline. A large part of southern Louisiana, then, is made up of deposits from elsewhere. That process has slowed dramatically in recent geological times, but the Mississippi even now is responsible for a deposit of approximately half a million tons of sediment every day.[1] These deposits have created an immense swath of wetlands reaching from New Orleans to the Gulf Coast that now include some three and a half million acres of swamps and marshes.[2] The land is soft and unstable underfoot, shifting almost whimsically from something firm and steady to something moist and sodden, and then, without warning, to water. It is an ever-evolving fusion of sea and land.

For those living north of the wetlands—the residents of New Orleans being a prominent example—the terrain just south of them serves as an important buffer zone that provides a line of defense against hurricanes and other storm events that gather energy out in the waters of the Gulf and then move inland. The plant life that flourishes in these wetlands—a fragile mixture of marsh soil and fresh water—serves as a kind of shock absorber, blunting these rude intrusions. Both the soil and the water flow southward from lands to the north, and both are resistant to surges of deadly saltwater from the sea, a point we revisit later in this chapter. It takes sturdy roots for plant life to survive in surroundings like these, and wetland plants have learned through the process of evolution over the millennia the importance of reaching deep into the ground below when storms threaten. But these deep-rooted plants have been withering and disappearing rapidly of late.

THE LANDSCAPE THAT HUMANS MADE

That delicate composition of elements has been disintegrating right before our eyes for quite some time, in large part because so many human settlers have been reshaping the natural landscape to make it more orderly, more logical, more rational, and, of course, more profitable.

Beginning in the 1700s and during the centuries that followed, the leaders of New Orleans focused a good deal of their available resources on cutting canals across the surface of the land in order to rearrange the region's waterways, extract natural resources, and improve commerce. We will not go further into this important chapter in the history of New Orleans except to note that this same longing to reshape the flows of water across the surface of the land was not confined to the inner waterways of the city but reached out into the broader countryside. The historical record gives us a good sense of how the civic leaders of New Orleans and the state of Louisiana thought about the way nature had formed the local landscape. When progress in engineering allowed the building of the Industrial Canal, the governor of Louisiana observed that "commerce seeks the channel of least resistance"; if New Orleans was to enjoy "the great advantages" provided to the city by nature, he added, then "man must come to its assistance."[3] At the time, the city and the state were beginning to envision the digging of the Mississippi River Gulf Outlet (MRGO), which would slice that channel all the way from New Orleans to the Gulf. The *New Orleans Item* editorialized that the "port's lifeline should not depend entirely upon a crooked, fog-covered, silt-bearing, temperamental river channel, which might otherwise restrain or restrict the growth of the port of New Orleans."[4]

Human engineering has often turned to straight lines where curves seem to have been nature's own way, and that certainly appears to have been the case in New Orleans and across the Louisiana wetlands. In both settings, waterways were cut as straight as the land's surface would allow, on the sensible theory that the fastest way for water vessels to journey from one place to another would be to travel in a straight line. Logical. But, alas, the same logic applies in reverse. It is also the case that storm surges, violent gusts of wind, and other natural threats to human safety are best served by those same straight lines. Surges of water, like floating vessels, are drawn to the most direct channel and for exactly the same reason: that channel is the fastest and most efficient way to reach distant targets. Experts who fully understood this, and who warned us well in advance, were largely ignored.[5] Katrina (and other hurricane events before and since) vindicated these experts in a way that is not likely to be forgotten anytime soon.

So the wetlands were slowly becoming a vast network of canals, channels, and other human-built waterways—kept securely in place by a vast system of levees and floodwalls—in order to improve on the ways of nature in the name of "progress." We can add dam construction to that frightening list, particularly along the Mississippi River and its tributaries. Those dams sharply reduced the deposit of sediment from the American hinterland on which the wetlands depended for survival.

The crowning blow may well have been the discovery of oil in the region in 1901. This led to the drilling of tens of thousands of exploratory and developmental wells into the uncertain soils of the wetlands; the slicing of more efficient pathways for the barges and other craft used to explore the terrain for sources of oil and gas; and then, of course, the extraction of oil and gas when the search was successful.[6] Extraction required that large chunks of the surfaces of the land be torn away, not only to dig wells but also to dig trenches for underground pipelines, dredge canals to allow equipment access, and the like. These rearrangements of the terrain accomplished their intended purpose of increasing the available supply of oil and gas and enriching the bank accounts of those who did the rearranging. But they also had the unintended consequence of further weakening the wetlands, which were quite literally being ripped out by their roots. It is worth underscoring that some who sought that intended result did so in full knowledge that they were helping to bring about ecological destruction. Ivor van Heerden noted clearly:

> Our wetlands are the nation's number-one source of crude oil (pumping more than the Alaska pipeline) and the second-leading source of natural gas, and in order to support and transport this production the companies have carved, by one calculation, 8,000 miles of cuts and canals throughout the wetlands. Since this entire network ties into the Gulf of Mexico, it provides opportunity for saltwater encroachment. It is subject to erosion and disrupts the natural flow of waters in the marshes. The whole artificial system works to the detriment of the wetlands. No one claims otherwise.[7]

This brings us back to the inevitable topic of the MRGO cutting right through the heart of the wetlands. The outlet certainly deserves its place at the center of attention when the subject turns to the dissolution of the wetlands and the effects on New Orleans and the rest of the countryside, having been so important a contributor to that outcome. But it is also an appropriate focus of our attention because it serves so well as a concentrated portrayal of the misjudgments and other grave errors that characterized the whole human effort to reshape the wetlands.

Construction of the outlet began in 1958 and was declared complete in 1965. The initial excavation involved the removal of close to 300 million cubic yards of dirt, far more than was required for the completion of the Panama Canal, and even that staggering amount soon turned out to be little more than the first few shovelfuls of what would later have to be removed to keep the outlet in motion.[8] It was "straight as an engineer's ruler," as one commentator put it, and that turned out to be a major problem.

A good deal of thoughtful criticism was directed at the decision to begin this project, as pointed out earlier. Well before the construction project began, a "Statement of Concern" by the Louisiana Wildlife and Fisheries Commission warned that "highly valuable and irreplaceable fish and wildlife resources and areas" were likely to be fatally damaged.[9] About a year later, as the project opened, an interim report from the US Department of the Interior noted that the marshes through which the channel was to be sliced were very valuable and warned that the excavation could result in major ecological change with widespread and severe consequences for the natural environment.[10]

Part of the problem was that the "outlet"—a flow of water following the laws of gravity and making its way directly toward the sea—was also a perfect "inlet" for saltwater intrusion in times of turmoil. Surges from the sea brought inland a level of salinity that had drastic consequences for the local plant life. The Mississippi River Gulf Outlet first earned the nickname "Hurricane Highway" in 1965, forty years before Katrina, when Hurricane Betsy used that handy opening to force its way inland much farther than had been expected. Not long afterwards, it earned the nickname "Hurricane Alley" as well. Ivor van Heerden and his colleagues describe the outlet as "an excellent storm-surge delivery system" that the federal powers-that-be had inadvertently designed.[11] It is not hard to imagine that Katrina, pausing for a moment to scan the horizon for a suitable place to land, noticed an open gap on the flank of the coastline that offered a corridor of unprotected wetlands aimed as straight as a rifle barrel right at New Orleans. Hurricanes are not widely known for their ability to think things through like that, so this suggestion will have to rank as whimsy. As it turned out, however, Hurricane Highway lived up to its name.

We described the wetlands earlier as a delicate balance of water and soil. The first of those two ingredients, of course, is *fresh water*, flowing downward with the Mississippi River and spreading out across southern Louisiana. The wetlands thrive on fresh water and know nothing more malignant than the *saltwater* that flows upward from the Gulf. Salinity is fatal to the plants of the region, save for those that have evolved to live in brackish water. The loss of native plant life is problematic for many reasons, including the importance of their presence to keeping the fragile soil in place. Cypress trees are particularly important in this respect: their tough roots reach deep down into the underground and stabilize what would otherwise be soggy mud, if not open water. In the absence of nourishing fresh water, cypress trees simply give up, their irreplaceable roots withering and losing their grip.

Virtually all of the rearranging of that landscape undertaken by human hands over the years—the canals and channels and other waterways cut across the surfaces of the land; the oil and gas industry's reshaping of the natural vista as an aid to exploration and extraction; and that gaping wound, that insult to nature, the Mississippi River Gulf Outlet—has turned out to be an open invitation to saltwater to make its way farther and farther inland. Upon its completion, the MRGO offered a shortcut to saltwater intrusion, as our whimsical Katrina understood all too well.

It can be difficult sometimes to avoid getting lost in a statistical fog when reflecting on what happened to the Louisiana wetlands when human engineers went to work on them. The most stunning evidence is found in the sheer volume of loss. Vast stretches of what once was fertile, productive land became more and more saturated as time passed and finally dissolved into open water. Far saltier than before, the wetlands water has made the ecosystem even more difficult to restore, and the wetlands have been slipping away at a rate of 25 to 35 square miles per year for the last half-century.[12] Researchers calculate that the wetlands are being lost at a rate of one US football field every sixty minutes, which is the equivalent of two to three square miles every month and 30 square miles every year—a portion of land the size of Manhattan.[13] Roughly one million acres of those wetlands have vanished in the last few decades.[14] That is equivalent to what the mighty Mississippi has deposited in those territories over the past one thousand years. The remaining wetlands are in danger of shrinking further, if not disappearing altogether.[15] John Barry offers yet another way to calculate the dimensions of that loss: "This protective buffer took six thousand years to form," yet "it has been brought to the brink of destruction in a lifetime."[16]

All these numbers can be hard to take in, but they make it clear that the wetlands are literally disappearing as we watch it happen. It is not an existing condition we are speaking of here so much as a rapid, ongoing motion. Not so much an event as a continuum.

One of many devastating consequences of the destruction of the wetlands is the loss of that shock absorber, the buffer zone that has been protecting human settlements located farther inland from weather events surging up from the seawaters below. For centuries now, this has been a basic reality in that part of the world. New Orleans in particular is now far more vulnerable and exposed than it has been at any time in its past, and unless weather patterns or human habits change dramatically, that will also remain a basic reality.[17] It is widely assumed by specialists that the storm surge generated by Katrina on its way north made it as far inland as it did only because the wetlands below were so battered that they yielded and simply gave up.

One reliable estimate is that the MRGO was responsible for the destruction or at least the severe degradation of 65,000 acres of wetlands (something close to 100 square miles)—all for the single purpose of helping vessels make their way to the sea a bit faster. William Freudenberg and his fellow sociologists wrote that, "without the loss of those miles of marshes and cypress swamps, the storms that hit the city might have been several feet lower.... In a very real sense, MRGO proved to be the single cut that led to a thousand deaths."[18]

The lasting irony of that effort is that the outlet, for all practical purposes, was on the verge of obsolescence by the time it was completed. The original idea was to cut a channel through the center of the wetlands 625 feet wide and 36 feet deep to accommodate large vessels on their way to and from the Gulf. An expectation like that, however, could only be realized if the edges of the excavation, the banks of what would soon become the waterway, could be counted on to remain intact. But the saltwater invited into the interior of the wetlands by the same excavation soon led to the death of the cypress trees and other vegetation that had kept the local soil firm enough for that purpose. Before too long, then, the banks of the channel turned into soft sludge and slumped down into the excavation, which of course seriously decreased both the width and depth of the channel. As a result, an almost continual process of dredging was required simply to keep the outlet functioning. The costs of that proved to be staggering.

Before long, the crumbling of the land on either side of the channel widened it to half a mile in some places, ten times the size of the initial excavation. In the meantime, a further complication was that well over 90 percent of the vessels leaving New Orleans for the Gulf continued to use the Mississippi River to get there, notwithstanding its "temperamental" and "crooked" ways.[19] In 2004, one year before Katrina, fewer than a dozen round trips were recorded on the MRGO, bringing the cost of each trip up to an absurd $1.5 million.[20] Something had gone very wrong there. To bring this sad tale to an even more mournful end, the US Army Corps of Engineers, responsible for the construction of the MRGO, has since acknowledged not only that the channel is almost useless in its present condition but that it cannot be filled in now.[21] The canal itself will remain a permanent gash on the countryside and an ever-widening pathway inland for storm surges from future hurricanes.

After reviewing that record, when should we say that "Katrina" actually began in historical time? That is no easy matter, we have to conclude. What is clear is that Katrina can no longer be conceptualized as an "event" with an easily identified beginning and an easily identified end, as Aristotle's rules for drama require. It has to be seen as yet another current in the continuing flows of ongoing history, understandable only by tracing that current back in time, as we have been doing here, and then ahead in time, which shall be our next subject.[22]

THE END?

No one familiar with disasters is likely to declare that the story of Katrina has come to a close and is now over and done with. But virtually every effort we make to measure the damage done to the landscape or to the people living on its terrain must fit into a bounded span of time, as we do when we calculate the costs of war. The death toll we arrive at is a count of the combatants who lost their lives in hostilities that took place between the moment the war is reckoned to have begun and the moment it is reckoned to have ended—the moment of a surrender or cease-fire or some other phenomenon that is measurable in time. The number of deaths and injuries ascribed to Katrina are similarly influenced by when we say that Katrina began and when we say it ended.

COUNTING THE DEAD

Anyone asking for the official death toll from Katrina in the years following it would have been given a precise number. At one point it was 1,833.[23] That was the total number of persons who were thought to have been crushed, drowned, or killed in some other way by the winds, floodwaters, or other extreme conditions caused by Katrina. For a long time afterward, a body would be discovered here or there—under a pile of debris, curled into a dark corner somewhere, stretched out on an attic floor that had been submerged under water—and the death count would go up by one. No bell rang, but the effect was the same.

The point that needs to be made here is that counting the dead in this way amounts to an almost meaningless form of arithmetic. The official death toll of Katrina does not include all the people who are *known* to have died as a result of the disaster and the protracted recovery process that followed. For example, suicide rates went up sharply in New Orleans and elsewhere over the months and even years that followed Katrina.[24] Suicides are hardly ever counted among official disaster-related deaths, however, and that would have been the case here even if the suicide had been accompanied by a note naming Katrina as its cause.

Everyone in New Orleans knew, or knew of, people who belonged on that tragic roster. Persons who simply gave up, victims of misery, neglect, and sheer weariness; persons who lost the support of a sustaining communal circle and did not know how to keep going in its absence; persons who drank themselves to death; persons who veered off the side of a dark road at night taking chances they would never have taken before; persons who stopped taking what they knew to be life-sustaining medication because they just did not care anymore.

A local journalist who had seen more than most humans are even able to imagine drove his car into a police barricade one day in the expectation (or the hope?) that he would simply be shot dead. That harsh outcome, now sometimes referred to as "suicide by cop," did not happen that day, maybe because those officers had seen enough themselves to realize what was going on. What if the journalist's desperate stratagem had been successful? That death would not have entered the record as a casualty of Katrina.

For nearly a decade after Katrina, the anthropologist Katherine Browne traced the post-disaster recovery process of the members of a very large group of relatives known locally as the Johnson-Fernandez family.[25] One of the pillars of that family, Katie, was part of an expansive web of kin who evacuated together to Dallas during the storm and then returned to St. Bernard Parish together in the months after. As Katie and her family worked to reestablish their cultural traditions, they also struggled to navigate the complicated private insurance and governmental recovery bureaucracy. In December 2007, just prior to the holidays, Katie, who was missing a leg due to complications from diabetes and had been denied the FEMA trailer for persons with disabilities that she requested, learned that her Road Home settlement—the program that promised to help Louisiana citizens rebuild after Katrina and Rita—would be less than half what she expected.[26] When Browne asked Katie why she had not begun her usual decorating for the holidays, she ruefully replied, "I'm too blue. I don't see no light on the horizon." A few days later, Katie experienced a massive stroke. She led a diminished life for years after the stroke and eventually died in 2013, but Katie is not counted among the roster of the Katrina dead. Should she be?

The carefully time-bounded way of thinking about counting disaster deaths really does defy logic—or at least what we would want to define as *socio*-logic. To limit the death toll to those killed in a raging storm has the virtue of placing them in easily circumscribed locations in space and time, and that, of course, would be an impossible task if we continued to count deaths that occur as time moves ahead into an ongoing and uncertain future. Indeed, the latter method would be a very untidy way to calculate a death toll, but to do otherwise takes away the real meaning of those deaths. They are not "aftermaths," as storytellers and historians sometimes suggest—occurrences well after an event. They are the essential elements of the story itself.

That is how the dead are counted. The same is true for the wounded.

Many of those who made it out of New Orleans alive became the walking wounded. The Centers for Disease Control and Prevention reported that thousands of survivors suffered from "non-fatal health-related issues" and other injuries *after* Katrina.[27] It is also important to note that a number of these same persons suffered from alarmingly high rates of chronic medical conditions *before* the hurricane made landfall.[28]

Those many already vulnerable residents who were unable to evacuate before Katrina made landfall, as well as those who chose to ride out the storm, were stuck in 90-degree temperatures and stifling humidity for days. Some were badly dehydrated or suffering from heat exhaustion by the time help finally arrived. Many others ended up wading through waist- or even chest-deep floodwaters as they sought higher ground. Along the way, many people got cuts, scrapes, bruises, and bumps. The medical status of some residents deteriorated rapidly because their open wounds were exposed to the toxic brew that submerged the streets of New Orleans.

Every calculable rate of mental illness went up in the months and years

FIGURE 3.1. Katrina survivors in the Ninth Ward navigate the murky floodwaters. Photo © Charlie Varley/varleypix.com, 2005.

following Katrina, and every scrap of evidence from news reports, field studies, and other sources suggested the same. As the nation paused to observe the second anniversary of the hurricane, the rates of depression and anxiety and other forms of trauma among survivors were higher than they had been two months after the storm.[29] And what should one make of the fact that, as the third anniversary approached, they were higher still?

Some of the most knowledgeable experts on the subject, including many of the nation's leading psychiatrists and psychologists, turned to the standard clinical diagnostic term, "post-traumatic stress disorder," and gave those symptoms the name "delayed-onset post-traumatic stress disorder." If we pause for a moment to make out what such an awkward arrangement of words actually means, it can only be that the people who are now suffering from traumatic injuries are reacting to irritants that took place two, three, even four years earlier. A similar logic would be at work in someone diagnosed as suffering from a "delayed-onset headache"—meaning that the discomfort that person feels right now is not a reaction to something that happened this morning or yesterday or the day before that, but something that happened two or three years earlier, though it is not yet recognized. Similarly, a person's nervous system may, for some reason, be slow to notice or to respond to a blow to the head or to other parts of the body that actually took place years ago.

This is a strange terminology, we would suggest, and a strange form of either medicine or psychology. It matters for a reason we have been drawing attention to throughout this discussion. What that terminology is suggesting, without quite saying so explicitly, is that a person's current discomfort is a response, not to things that took place in the present, but to some lingering trace of something that took place in the past. This terminology does not take into account the current distress of a New Orleans resident as a reaction to the loss of faith in the larger social order, or to the wrenching disruptions of everyday life in a land trying to recover from a disaster, or to an ever-deeper fall into poverty, despair, hopelessness, or exile.

This way of drawing a conclusion fails to recognize what the evidence we have in hand is trying so hard to point out to us. If someone suffers from a traumatic reaction two or three years *after* a disaster is reckoned to be over, the only logical deduction is that the original calculation was inaccurate. The disaster is not over. It is ongoing, and the present symptoms are clear evidence of that fact.[30]

*　　*　　*

As this chapter comes to a close, it should be made clear that there are very good reasons for locating disasters and other disturbing events in distinct segments of time—both for the sake of history and for the sake of personal and societal healing. But that kind of realization can come at a cost. A decade after Katrina, the journalist Katy Reckdahl wrote that the city still had "few unqualified victories," and she mused that perhaps the state of things could best be characterized as *recovery with an asterisk*.[31] Reckdahl recognized that, as we have tried to argue here, assigning counts and placing bookends on events that are ongoing for the people wounded by them comes at a real human cost.

Those of us who look in on a disaster from a vantage point well outside it are doing so with eyes focused quite differently than those of survivors who may still be caught up in it. We outsiders may find it fairly easy to frame the event, to give it a distinct location in time and space. But it is important to appreciate that survivors are almost certain to be looking at a different scene, one that better fits the realities of their circumstances. Many of them are still in a struggle with the dark currents that surge so relentlessly and so painfully around them. When we close off our calculations as to who and what constitutes a casualty of Katrina, and when we conclude that a person's current sufferings can best be understood as a delayed reaction to something that happened months or even years ago, we have lost our chance to understand their reality as well as a chance to be of better help to them. And that's no small matter.

IN SPACE

At the risk of sounding as though we are playing a sly game with words, we would propose that there are actually two separate entities that can reasonably be called "New Orleans." The first (and most obvious) of them is that parcel of land marked off by border lines and represented on official maps. After Katrina, virtually every word we heard from city, state, and federal officials who drew plans to restore the harm done spoke to *that* New Orleans. It is the one measurable in square miles.

But there is another way to envision a city, one that social scientists have been weighing for a long time, and that is to think of it as a living organism.[1] The cells of that organism are the individual persons who make it up. The metabolism of that organism is the way those cells interact with one another. The social and cultural temper of that organism is the patterning of everyday life among the cells that constitute it. Thinking that way, it is not too hard to imagine that those human cells—the forces that gave the organism shape, tone, and character—continued to be the New Orleans of 2005, even when harsh winds and lashing waters drove them elsewhere. After all, it was *they* who lived in that space, *they* who absorbed the assault on the organism, *they* who carry the wounds.

Both of these versions of New Orleans were shattered by Katrina and its surreal aftermath. But it makes an immense difference whether talk about "restitution" or "rebuilding" or "reconstruction" or "recovery" refers to those acres of land that are identified on the official city map as, for instance, "the Lower Ninth Ward" or to those tens of thousands of people who *were* the Lower Ninth in the sense that they belonged to it, gave it form, and constituted its history. It is very reasonable to think of *that* Lower Ninth as the *real* Lower Ninth. It still exists, but its parts are to be found in other locations in Louisiana as well as in Houston, Atlanta, San Antonio, and elsewhere across the country.

The simple fact is that billions of dollars were set aside to restore the first New Orleans and almost none for the second. That matters in the first instance because so many of those people who were driven off into distant places continue to regard themselves as being a natural part of the New Orleans they are separated from—as a part of its living tissue. It matters in the second instance because almost no voices from that other New Orleans were being heard in the councils that decided what was to happen in the place they continued to think of as home.

It will come as little surprise if we add that the people being left out in that definition of New Orleans were, in large part, Black, living below the poverty line, and, by a wide margin, the New Orleanians most likely to have experienced serious loss and suffering from Katrina. They left their home city as evacuees as a result of the storm. Something like 100,000 of them had not returned years later.[2] Many never will.

As of now, much of the Lower Ninth Ward is a bleak, open space. Gary Rivlin thought that it looked and felt like a "moonscape" a decade after Katrina.[3] Those who visit that moonscape in a proper frame of mind, their senses tuned in the right way, can almost *hear* the voices and *feel* the sorrow of the people who lived in those now empty spaces so recently. Their presence is palpable. We do not want to strike too theatrical a note here or change something so painful into a tragic dramatic scene, but we do want to point out that a good part of the *soul* of the Lower Ninth and a good part of what was once New Orleans—and in that other sense still *is* New Orleans—is now spilled all over the place.

A PLACE ON THE MAP

We focus first on "New Orleans" in the way cartographers do—as a contained space on the surface of the land. From there, we turn to a tracing of the powerful forces that shaped the boundaries of inclusion and exclusion in the city. After Katrina, it was apparent right from the start that leading citizens of the city as well as developers from outside it sensed an opportunity in the misery surrounding them. Prospects for the future would be vastly improved for them if most of the evacuees then leaving the city (in particular the poorer and darker and most likely to vote Democratic among them) elected not to return or were prevented from doing so.[4] These forces, in other words, planned for a New Orleans in which something like one-quarter of the individual cells that made up the urban body at that time had been surgically removed.

As Gary Rivlin prepared his book on Katrina, he turned often to Lance Hill, a widely respected observer of the civic culture of New Orleans. "It was impossible not to pick up on this sentiment that this was our chance to take back control of the city," Hill said. "There was virtually a near consensus among Whites that authorities should not do anything to make it easy for poor African Americans to come back."[5] That clearly became unwritten policy among the city leadership as well as among important state and federal contributors to the "recovery" effort. Rivlin also wrote of the time when

a contingent of 55 Michigan State troopers had volunteered to help in the Gulf Coast after Katrina. They were asked to assist the police in Baton Rouge, where multiple officers said they were under orders: make life unpleasant for New Orleans evacuees so that they would relocate elsewhere. One trooper quoted a local cop's reference to Blacks as "animals" who needed to be "beaten down." As a thank-you gift, another trooper said, he was invited to "beat down" a man in custody. A small squadron of state troopers from New Mexico also assigned to Baton Rouge told a similar story. A complaint the New Mexico commander filed with the city stated that his people had witnessed illegal searches, physical abuse, and other behavior that a troop official summed up as "racially motivated."[6]

Andrew A. Beveridge, an expert in demography and a frequent social analyst for the *New York Times*, summarized things five years after Katrina: "Though it is very difficult to get data that looks directly at change, nonetheless three broad conclusions can be reached." Those include:

First. African Americans and the poor were the most seriously affected by the flood… and serious remedial measures would be necessary to make them whole. This has not happened.

Second. The displacement of many Black people and the poor was welcomed by a variety of government officials. Indeed, policies were enacted and actions were taken to make it particularly difficult for low-income individuals (who were more likely to be African American) to return. This despite the fact that almost all displaced low-income tenants preferred to return to New Orleans.

Third, the racial composition of New Orleans is still very different from that before Katrina, and given the housing and other policies, the likelihood is that the city will remain vastly different from the way it was before the flood.[7]

Those hopes for a whiter, wealthier future were echoed up and down the halls of the most powerful places in New Orleans, and then, when the sought-after demographic shifts began to happen, those outcomes were widely applauded behind closed doors. Andrew Horowitz offers a sampling of comments that made their way from those halls into the public record:

"The hurricane drove poor people and criminals out of the city, and we hope they don't come back," a New Orleans realtor told a reporter.

"The party is finally over for these people…and now they're going to have to find someplace else to live."

"Those who want to see this city rebuilt want to see it done in a completely different way: demographically, geographically, and politically," a wealthy White resident of unflooded Uptown told the *Wall Street Journal*.[8]

David Brooks of the *New York Times* joined the conversation by recommending that the best available opportunity for New Orleans was to relocate the poor elsewhere not only for the sake of the crippled city but for what he supposed would be the well-being of the individual evacuees.[9] A decade after Katrina, Malcolm Gladwell, writing for *The New Yorker*, claimed that the forced relocation of tens of thousands of low-income Black people following Katrina was a positive thing because it opened up the possibility for upward mobility.[10] None of these observers were taking into account the human costs of people not only being wrenched away from the land they saw themselves as rooted in, but also realizing that their fellow townspeople were sending them into exile.

Politics played a prominent role in the decision of the city leaders that they would be better served if many of the evacuees did not return at all. New Orleans has been widely described as a blue dot on a red political landscape, and the voting habits of African American residents of the city could make a difference in the outcome of state and even federal elections.[11] After Katrina, the civil liberties of displaced Black residents were left unprotected as Republican lawmakers steadily chipped away at key aspects of the 1965 Voting Rights Act.[12] Kathleen Blanco was the Democratic governor of that otherwise deeply red state at the time of Katrina, and almost as if to prove a point, Bobby Jindal, a Republican, was elected governor in 2008 while some sixty thousand Black voters were looking for ways to return home.[13] That election outcome was the *new* New Orleans making itself felt across the state and the nation.

The decision of the leadership of New Orleans to "take back control of the city" was unambiguously expressed in a decision by the New Orleans City Council to systematically demolish four major public housing developments. They fenced them off and then flattened 4,600 units without allowing former residents—nearly all of whom were African American—to revisit them or even to reclaim their own furnishings and other belongings.[14] Those who attempted to do so were threatened with arrest.[15] Cindi Katz, a sociologist from New York, saw those public housing units before they were completely demolished and was struck by the fact that they were "locked and barricaded." She wrote: "Seeing those barely damaged developments behind chain link fences topped with barbed wire, all of their entry ways covered with steel plates, was one of the most shocking things I saw during my visit to the city."[16]

The demolished public housing was replaced with federally funded complexes that required the city to follow mixed-use redevelopment models.

FIGURE 4.1. A child's toy sits behind a fence at one of the public housing units slated for demolition in New Orleans. Photo © Lori Peek, 2008.

The official logic being applied here was to destroy and then replace those public housing units with housing for mixed-income families. This is an appealing idea at first glance, in that the developments would allow people of different backgrounds, different incomes, different life prospects, and, of course, different racial groups to gather communally. An urban village green. Democracy in action.

But no one was fooled. It was yet another measure to keep poor and Black persons from returning. Lance Hill put it bluntly to the *New York Times*: "The people who have been planning the recovery process never wanted poor people to return to the city in the first place."[17] Congressman Richard Baker of Louisiana, quoted in the *Wall Street Journal*, said: "We finally cleaned up public housing in New Orleans. We couldn't do it, but God did."[18]

Several members of our research team, including the two of us, stood on a sidewalk within a few feet of one of those public housing complexes watching immense, elaborate pieces of machinery with huge steel teeth chew their way down a block-long public housing complex, reducing everything before it—household furnishings from the inside and sturdy brick walls from the outside—into a crushed layer of debris. The forward movement of that equipment as it made its way down the row of apartments was fast enough to be visible from the street for passers-by who paused for more than a few minutes. We were joined on the sidewalk by two African American women, former residents of the complex, who were there to watch what was once their home being ground into small shards and strewn across the ground. Their faces were drawn, reflecting a kind of resigned anguish.

The cascading list of measures taken by city leaders to prevent the return of poor and Black fellow citizens could go on for pages. For example, over 7,500 public school teachers and paraprofessionals, mostly African American women, were fired after Katrina when the state of Louisiana took over the already troubled school system.[19] A decade after the storm, nine out of ten New Orleans public schools had been privatized as part of the extended charter school experiment. Charity Hospital, the one facility in the city with the mission to provide health care to the poor and uninsured, was flooded in Katrina. Despite the heroic efforts of hospital staff and military personnel to reopen the facility, state officials—eager to garner federal funds to support the construction of a new medical complex—announced that Charity Hospital would be permanently shuttered on September 30, 2005.[20] Kristina Kay Robinson, a local artist and activist, captured the harsh realities of life in New Orleans: "To remain in the city

FIGURE 4.2. Demolition of public housing in New Orleans.
Photo © Lori Peek, 2008.

has required a quick recovery, an erasure with no mourning. No truth or recompense for what has been lost and what was taken. No admission of what we all know to be true: that the worst results of Hurricane Katrina have had nothing to do with Mother Nature."[21]

The result of these various official actions is clear. Evacuees who thought they were being transported out of immediate danger and onto safer ground for a short period of time after Katrina were actually being offered one-way tickets out of town. It quickly became obvious to all who were paying attention that return tickets would never be issued and that "welcome home" messages would not be posted on the roads pointing toward New Orleans. The evacuation had become a Black diaspora.[22]

Meanwhile, more than four thousand newcomers per year moved into the city—most of them economically comfortable, most of them White—and in many ways by local standards things were looking up. The question then became: For whom? Those who found themselves a long way from home and beginning to suspect that they had been exiled knew the answer. When Kalamu ya Salaam, a local author, was asked if New Orleans could "come back better" after Katrina, he replied "No." A "better city" can only mean that "all the people who were here before could come back as something else."[23] Cells returning to the original body.

That is what the scene looked like from that place on the map known as New Orleans in the months and years following Katrina. The mostly unwritten policy had clearly worked. The results of that urban strategy are hard to quantify, since the available figures bounce around so much, but it is reasonable to conclude that only 10 percent of the persons evicted from those public housing developments were able to find lodging in the new apartments built on those renovated sites, and that something like 50 percent of them never returned to the city at all.[24] Adding together other efforts to reduce the availability of affordable public housing, Gary Rivlin concludes that the city had fourteen thousand public housing units for the poor in the 1990s but that there were fewer than three thousand in 2015, ten years after Katrina.[25] If we make a guess that those units would have housed an average of four persons apiece, that is a drop of roughly forty-five thousand individuals, a number approaching one-tenth of the pre-Katrina population of New Orleans.

We have every reason to suppose that all those persons, dislodged so abruptly from what was their natural milieu, their home-land, felt that they had been torn from their native turf. We wrote in chapter 1 that the people of the Louisiana wetlands tend to assume that they belong to— literally *belong* to—the terrain surrounding them, and they feel dislodged when swept away by whatever fates carry them elsewhere.

It is almost an irony to then suggest that the same can be said for a vast majority of the people of New Orleans. The sounds and sights of the activities on the streets of the city seem, at first glance, to reflect as urban a landscape as can easily be imagined. But experienced hands are quick to note that residents' sense of attachment to that metropolitan space and those crowded sidewalks is very similar to what one sees and hears and feels in neighboring rural territories.[26] For one thing, a vast majority of the residents of New Orleans either were born in the city itself or moved in from the nearby countryside, so they are essentially products of the same regional culture. For another thing, as urbane as New Orleans appears to be in spirit, it resembles a rural village in ways that few if any other metropolitan sites in this country could. Dan Baum expresses it particularly well: "In general, when New Orleanians describe what they love most about the city, the first thing they mention is neither the food nor the music but the intimacy of the neighborhoods—knowing everybody on the block where you were born, and never leaving."[27]

New Orleans is a city of neighborhood clusters, very much like the rest of Louisiana. Elizabeth Fussell has pointed out elsewhere that, before Katrina, nearly 80 percent of New Orleans residents were born in Louisiana and had lived most of their lives there.[28] This is far above the average for urban places in the United States. These residents were torn away from lands in which they felt rooted—lands in which they felt fully human and truly alive.

One of the present authors, Kai Erikson, once interviewed a group of migrant farm workers from Haiti with the help of a young anthropologist who spoke Creole well and was serving as interpreter. One of the early questions Erikson asked was the all too familiar: "Where are you from?" He knew just enough French to realize that the interpreter was saying something quite different in Creole, and when he inquired about that, he was told: "I know what you are trying to find out, but you are putting the matter poorly. I am asking 'where are you a person'?" That's it exactly. Where are you at home? Where do you draw your strength from? Where do you feel truly human?

Those persons displaced from Louisiana and elsewhere were torn loose from a human landscape in which they felt at home and protected by layers of insulation that only kin and a nourishing community can supply. In doing so, they suffered a blow every bit as harsh as the storm itself and the collapse of the levees that followed. Later indications were unmistakable. The dislocated suffered from the fearful things that had happened to them. And as the years passed, they faded further and further out of sight in the blurs of time.

III

KATRINA AS HUMAN EXPERIENCE

Many of the people caught in the throes of Katrina can be said to have experienced three different concussions—blows to the mind and spirit. The earliest blow came from the severe deprivations and other torments that so many African Americans and low-income people in the New Orleans area had been exposed to earlier in their lives. The second resulted from the pounding of the storm itself and the response that immediately followed. And then, third, to make things more painful yet, those people who had already suffered the most in the hurricane and flooding were more likely to experience what may well have been the bitterest blow of all. They were all but banished from the places they called home, not only by distant officials but by their fellow residents.

"Concussion" is a useful term to apply here because it is a well-known medical finding that a second concussion is likely to do far more damage to the victim than the first one did, never mind a third. Those outcomes cannot be calculated by simply adding the effects of a first blow to those of a second and then those of a third. Something closer to a form of multiplication must be used instead. It stands entirely to reason that people who go through such a sequence of events will be deeply numbed and even irrevocably damaged as a result.

We turn now to the final three chapters. While each focuses on a more or less distinct stretch of time—before Katrina, during Katrina, and after Katrina—our hope is to address the accumulation of assaults that accompanied each of those moments.

5

BEFORE
SEEKING OUT THE MOST VULNERABLE

Social scientists who follow disasters have noticed for quite some time now that survivors often view the natural forces closing in as aiming directly at them individually. For the most vulnerable who are so often in the path of these forces, it is easy to imagine that incoming disasters are actively probing the landscape, seeking out its softest flanks and the most marginal and least-defended people to be found there. Those people turn out so often to be the targets of incoming dangers that it is very common for them to wonder why they were singled out in this way. *Why us? Why here? Why now?* These are the questions asked by those who dwell in fishing villages along the coasts of Indonesia when a tsunami strikes, or by those who live in shantytowns on the outskirts of cities like Port-au-Prince when an earthquake does its crushing work.

William James, the great psychologist of another era, happened to be in the vicinity of San Francisco at the time of the deadly 1906 earthquake. He thought at first that the tremors reaching up from underneath the surface of the earth were pointed directly at him: "First, I personified the earthquake as a permanent individual entity.... It came directly... to *me*.... Animus and intent were never more present in any human action, nor did any human activity ever more definitely point back to a living agent as its source and origin." James, being a devoted inquirer into human behavior, interviewed several people in his immediate surroundings and then added to his report: "All whom I consulted on the point agreed to this feature in their experience."[1]

In Buffalo Creek, the site of a well-known flood in West Virginia in 1972, witnesses remembered thinking that the floodwaters were pursuing them like a living creature. "The water seemed like the demon itself. It came, destroyed, and left," said one survivor. Another looked back on the horror of it all: "I felt like the water was a thing alive and was coming after us to get us all. I still think of it as a live thing."[2]

The feeling that surging floodwaters or damaging winds or powerful tremors are "out to get us" is fairly common in disasters. Katrina was no different in that regard. A resident of Gentilly, a serene middle-class and predominantly African American neighborhood in the city's Eighth Ward, said, "I've never seen anything like this. The winds and water came to the city. It was like it came for us." Another New Orleanian said: "That water didn't knock or ring the bell. It chased me up the stairs, into the attic, and onto the roof. Water's not supposed to act like that! I could have sworn it was mad. At me."[3]

The irony here is that even though disaster survivors who reach such conclusions may not really see the underlying logic at work in what is happening to them, in a very important sense they are altogether correct in their assumptions. When we look from a reflective distance, it becomes obvious that the human population is spread out across the surfaces of the earth in such a way that the most disadvantaged among us are most likely to live in the riskiest places. We are not speaking here of disasters actively seeking out the vulnerable, of course. We are describing a nearly universal situation in which the socially and economically marginalized have already been herded into places where disasters are most likely to strike.[4] Tsunamis do not pick out the poor; the poor are pushed into those low-lying areas where the land meets the dangerous sea. Earthquakes do not seek out the ill-housed; they rupture along already existing fault lines but do the worst damage to fragile and shoddily built structures, the ones in which the needy have little choice but to dwell. Toxic wastes do not seek out the least-protected; they are deposited on the same parcels of land where the poor have already been deposited. And in the same way, Katrina's floodwaters did not seek out the poor; they had already been relegated to insecure locations—too often without access to private or public transportation or other means to enable evacuation.

We can go a step further in fact. If one were to draw a map of places worldwide in which disasters are most likely to strike, one would also be sketching at least an approximate map of places to which the poor are most likely to have been consigned.[5] This is not true all the time, but there is a clear correlation—to employ a term often used in the social sciences— to refer to a phenomenon observed frequently enough in everyday life to qualify as a stable social pattern. And there is no mystery to any of it. We need only ask: Who lives in secure dwellings, and who lives in tin shacks? Who lives along the bluffs, and who in the floodplains when volatile rivers overflow? Who lives near the corridor of chemical plants in Louisiana ominously named "Cancer Alley"? The list of such questions could be endless and can easily be applied to New Orleans in the time of Katrina.

As is so often the case, one can find prominent exceptions to the general rule. The well-off are known to deliberately place themselves in harm's way when they can afford the risk and there are benefits to be gained. For example, the frequent brushfires in the coastal hills of southern California appear to aim with deadly accuracy at the lavish dwellings of wealthy residents. In another example, many Scandinavian tourists were sunning themselves on the beaches of South Asia when the Indian Ocean tsunami of 2004 plunged ashore. But these sorts of exceptions do not disprove the general correlation between the location of the poor and the path of the deadliest of disasters. If anything, they serve to highlight it.

It is now a clearly established social fact of human life in our times that the poor suffer the most when disasters strike.[6] There is mounting evidence as well that disasters may deepen already existing inequalities, pushing struggling people even further into the depths of economic despair.[7] Laura Lein and her colleagues emphasize that disasters on the scale of Katrina can thrust the near-poor into "the basement of extreme poverty."[8]

To put it in a somewhat different way, disasters have a tendency to lash out at the already wounded—those who have experienced longtime exposure to poverty and discrimination; those have been treated as something less than fully human; and those who have suffered any of the other numbing disadvantages that can be described as sources of chronic traumatization, which can reach to the core of the human spirit just as harshly as acute forms of traumatization. These accumulations of disadvantage are something akin to slow-motion disasters.[9]

Finally, the feeling that an incoming disaster is actively seeking "us" out, pointing in "our" direction, is bound to be all the more terrifying and traumatizing for those who also sense that other human beings are after them as well. A good number of the African American residents of New Orleans, perhaps even a majority, are convinced that they were singled out in yet another way. It was actively guessed by residents of the Lower Ninth Ward that a few strategic levees were deliberately breached by city leaders so as to divert floodwaters from White neighborhoods into Black ones.[10] The available evidence does not support that dreaded suspicion in the case of Katrina, but if it sounds too far outside the realm of the possible, it is worth remembering that a similar stratagem is known to have been used during a storm in 1927.[11]

*   *   *

What follows is a brief detour to consider what the word "family" means to the people of New Orleans and the surrounding countryside who were the most badly wounded in body and in spirit by Katrina and its cruel aftermaths.

Anthropologists, sociologists, and other social scientists have been making a distinction for quite some time now between "nuclear" and "extended" types of family formations, and that distinction has gradually found its way into more general usage. A nuclear family in this context is composed of two parents and their immediate offspring, the assumption being that when the children mature they will leave that narrow inner fold and begin their own nuclear families. An extended family is an assembly of individuals who are related to one another genetically. It can include several generations of grandparents, parents, children, uncles, aunts, and cousins, as well as more distant bloodlines across social space. It can even include persons who are not genetically related at all but who are so closely connected that they feel and act like family and are thus included in what we call kin-hood.[12]

When specialists draw attention to the difference between "nuclear" and "extended" they are not dividing family formations into two distinct categories but instead are referring to differences spread across a continuum. The smallest unit that qualifies as "family," presumably, would be two, and we will soon refer to a close family grouping numbering in the low hundreds.

Whatever the original coiners of those terms had in mind, when "nuclear" and "extended" sit side by side on the printed page, they seem to suggest a kind of ranking. "Nuclear" implies essence, nucleus, base, while "extended" implies a broader reach beyond that central core into wider family circles. In everyday usage of those concepts in modern America, "nuclear" entities are assumed to be nature's way, while "extended" entities are thought of as a kind of protective network that people turn to when in need of wider support. People's lived experience is, of course, a good deal more complicated, but these are the baselines we begin with here.

Looking back into the past, it is clear that our species has experimented with different family patterns in order to adapt to shifting local and global circumstances. But it is a well-established fact that nuclear family forms became a good deal more common in the Western world about two hundred years ago, when a surge of industrialization and urbanization created a need for smaller and more mobile family units to migrate across the surfaces of the earth.

In the United States in more modern times, the assumption that nuclear families are the standard human arrangement was brought into public view in the 1960s and 1970s, when the press and politicians turned their attention to the ways of life they perceived to be taking place in the center of northern industrial cities like Chicago and Detroit. Most residents of those urban spaces were African Americans who had migrated from the rural South in recent years and had been accustomed for generations, even centuries, to a distinctly extended form of family composition.[13] A striking feature of that way of life to many commentators was the number of children "born out of wedlock" and raised in families headed by single women. To those onlookers, that bordered on the immoral and was a violation of both the natural and social order.

Senator Daniel Patrick Moynihan of New York, a prominent spokesperson in both the media and in politics back then, called what he thought he could see in those urban settings "a tangle of pathologies." Moynihan was far more concerned with disruptions to the social order than he was with the moral trespasses that troubled so many of his colleagues. He was deeply concerned that poor, Black, and badly abused citizens of the land were turning away from the nuclear option and in doing so failing to take advantage of the life strategy that he simply assumed was far and away the most likely to improve their future prospects. To him, it was a given that families headed by sturdy, competent, caring males were the human norm. A family without that basic anchor was taking the risk—sometimes a fatal risk—of going without the basic protection that the nuclear family could provide.

If one looks at Moynihan's written work on this subject, it becomes evident that either he knew very little about what social scientists and others were beginning to call "extended" family forms or he deliberately ignored the matter.[14] In his widely debated 1965 report, *The Negro Family: The Case for National Action*, Moynihan wrote that "the family structure of lower-class Negroes is highly unstable, and in many urban centers is approaching complete breakdown."[15] "Breakdown" clearly meant the failure of a "strong father figure." In the absence of that fundamental base, a family could be written off as "broken" or "illegitimate." Moynihan also argued that "ours is a society which presumes male leadership in private and in public affairs."[16] It is important to add, however, that he attempted to avoid assigning blame by acknowledging that the Black community "has paid a fearful price for the incredible mistreatment to which it has been subjected over the past three centuries."[17]

What Moynihan and others could not see with their intently focused perspective were the benefits that extended family groupings can offer young mothers and their offspring, whether or not a male spouse is part of the scene. At their best, such extended groupings can serve as a warm envelope of devoted people who can help protect each other from the disadvantages of being poor and Black. The large gathering of male and female relatives in an extended family can offer a range of comforts that smaller family units may not be able to provide. Those living in these groupings can be nourishing and affectionate with each other, and perhaps most important of all, they can share the pain when things go awry, not just the joys when all is well. In that sense, extended family groupings can be a profoundly rational way to adapt to the realities of an indifferent if not outright hostile social setting.[18]

Regardless of the importance of diverse family groupings, those heated discussions in the 1960s and 1970s had a lasting impact on the way this nation deals with familial structures. As we shall soon see, when Katrina charged ashore so abruptly some four decades later, both federal and state bureaucracies, with their rules and regulations, took it quite for granted that the badly damaged persons they were supposed to take care of lived in nuclear family units. To those rescuers, the primacy of the nuclear family structure was an established fact of American life.

When Katrina slammed into New Orleans in 2005, a good part of the city population had already fled town for safer terrain elsewhere. Most of the country and a good part of the rest of the world could see from news broadcasts who had been left behind to absorb the brunt of the assault. The visual evidence alone was staggering. The eye could see thick crowds of people pressed together at the Superdome and the Convention Center; survivors wading through three or four feet of dark, toxic floodwaters; and tight knots of people huddled together on highway overpasses and other elevated stretches of land looking desperately for some kind of help. What was easily learned from those scenes was that almost all of those who found themselves in immediate danger when the disaster hit were Black, poor, and, as we now know, very likely to be drawn to an extended type of family formation.[19]

Twenty-eight percent of the population of New Orleans lived below the poverty line and that more than half of those families were headed by single mothers with incomes averaging less than $20,000 a year.[20] Those statistics account for little more than one-quarter of the local population, a distinct minority, but in the end they described a very large proportion of those who were left in dangerous terrain when the disaster struck.[21]

Not long after Katrina visited New Orleans, one heard remarks similar to the ones so often made about the inner cities of the industrial North decades earlier. Jesse Jay Peterson, a widely quoted African American pastor from New Orleans, wrote that "it was the lack of moral character and dependence on government that cost Blacks when Hurricane Katrina struck, not President Bush or racism."[22] And George Will, a White commentator, suggested that it "is a safe surmise that more than 80 percent of African American births in inner-city New Orleans—as in some other cities—were to women without husbands. That translates into a large and constantly renewed cohort of lightly parented adolescent males, and that translates into chaos in neighborhoods and schools, come rain or come shine."[23]

We turn now to two anthropologists, Carol Stack and Katherine Browne, each of whom has spent many years in the field watching, listening to, and even joining family activities to better understand the social worlds they are studying. Stack's research, published in 1974, tells us of a community of Black migrants from the deep American South hoping to make a new life for themselves in the urban North while trying at the same time to recapture the cultural climate of their rural roots, a locale where "family" meant a wide spread of relatives and what we earlier called kin-hood.[24] That work scarcely mentions the terms "nuclear" and "extended" because those distinctions are simply not useful to Stack's subject.

Browne, who studied a large Black family numbering in the several scores and strongly rooted in the bayou communities outside New Orleans, observes that members of the family she came to know so well would be amazed to learn that social scientists sometimes make a distinction between nuclear and extended family structures. "No one called this big family an 'extended family,'" Browne notes, "because that would have suggested that there was some family unit that was not extended." She proposes that the family "has to be treated as a single living thing…not as the sum of discrete nuclear family households."[25] The family is a functioning organism, one might say, and its cells are the individual persons who make it up.

This brief discussion will have to end with a bitter conclusion. The extended family structure that turns out to be such an essential source of support in everyday life for the poor, people of color, and the otherwise disadvantaged can become a terrible handicap in a storm like Katrina, not only during its thunderous appearance on land, but just before it strikes and long after it has retreated.[26]

One threat that presented itself before Katrina came ashore was that extended family members did not have the flexibility of those in nuclear family structures to get out of harm's way. It makes a real difference if the family hoping to leave the danger zone is a relatively small cluster of parents, children, and perhaps a household pet or two, all of them fitting into a single vehicle that can set its sights on a motel or hotel that accommodates groups of just that size. But an extended family grouping is very likely to conclude that it is not really assembled, not really an intact body, until a certain number of individual households are ready to proceed together as one. The arrival of dangerous times almost by reflex calls for the gathering of the flock—the young, the old, the able, the infirm.

Larger families that did manage to evacuate together as Katrina approached had a limited range of destinations to choose from. Motel rooms and the like were all but out of the question for large groups, as a matter of cost as well as of size. The only alternatives out in that vast and often unwelcoming territory were mass shelters, the homes of relatives who lived outside of the disaster zone, or other accommodations that fate opened up in locations elsewhere. Those unable to evacuate could only brace themselves for the dangers about to land upon them.

As we noted in chapter 2, Michael Chertoff, the secretary of the Department of Homeland Security and the official in charge of the federal response, said after the storm: "The critical thing was to get people out before the disaster. Some people chose not to obey that order. It was a mistake on their part."[27] Michael Brown, the director of the Federal Emergency Management Agency (FEMA), following suit, said in response to a question posed about the rising death toll: "That's attributable to a lot of people…who chose not to leave."[28] Those remarks did not reflect any understanding at all of the social life of the people they had been assigned the responsibility of helping out. It was not that those people who failed to evacuate did not hear or understand or believe the urgency of the warnings they were receiving from those government authorities. They knew more about Gulf storms than those bureaucrats acknowledged, but they also had responsibilities that the leaders of those agencies could not seem to imagine. Consider, for example, one young woman who went to see her fifty-one-year-old mother-in-law who had been severely injured before the arrival of Katrina and had no way to get out of the city. The young woman said with distinct moral clarity: "I am not going to leave you…because I know you're here by yourself and don't have any way to get out.…So we're either going to get out together or we're going to be here together."[29] That woman, who was eventually able to help her mother-in-law flee the city with the assistance of other family members, was expressing the view of tens of thousands of her fellow citizens.

It should be evident by now why so many of those whom we have been calling extended family members remained in mortal danger. They could not evacuate on their own and leave the most vulnerable in their larger kin network—a single living organism—alone and helpless. Officials at the federal, state, and even city level had made no provisions at all for evacuation by plane or bus or any other form of transportation that could accommodate larger groups. Nor, for that matter, is there any evidence that they gave it a moment's thought. How many people lost their lives for just that reason will never be known.

6

DURING
BEING BATTERED BY THE STORM

A good part of this book so far has been devoted to the devastation of Katrina, but our focus has primarily been on what the damage looked like and how it influenced the reactions of federal and state officials and the media. We will turn now to what those moments spent in the storm itself felt like to those who endured them and how incidents like that can work their way into the core of each sufferer's inner being.

We begin this chapter by focusing on the experiences of persons who were exposed to the worst of Katrina's winds and waters and then to the assaults on them by subsequent events. Paying attention to those exposures helps us understand why disasters can be so damaging to the body and disturbing to the mind.

Katrina's power was terrifying for everyone caught in its path. The night before landfall, it seemed to many as if the intensifying hurricane-force winds were whistling an ominous prelude to the violent gusts and the deadly storm surges that would soon pay an unwelcome visit to the people of the Gulf Coast. As Katrina bore down, one man who had stayed behind said in awe, "I could stand on my back porch and scream at the top of my lungs and not hear myself."[1]

Hours later, as the day began to break, frantic phone calls for help overwhelmed the emergency phone lines in New Orleans. One of those operators dealt with the following exchanges in literally a matter of minutes: "Residence has collapsed," the operator said as she passed the information along to her supervisor shortly after 7:00 a.m., adding quickly, "Flooding inside." A moment later: "Female unable to breathe; she is oxygen-dependent." Next call: "House on fire." The furor continued:

"Another fire," and then, "Two males on roof," and "Water rising up to windows, people screaming that I'm drowning." The next call: "Elderly couple in a building. Roof came off."[2] This operator was but one of many then on duty.

Floodwaters eventually forced those emergency operators to abandon the 911 call center in the New Orleans police headquarters. But before their abrupt departure, the persons staffing the phone lines had assumed the grim task of informing stranded survivors that help was *not* on its way. Conditions were too dangerous to send emergency crews. "No, the police are not coming out until the weather conditions get better," one operator offered. "So I am going to die?" the caller said in response. "The water is steadily rising, ma'am, and I'm going to drown in the attic. I'm 37 years old!"[3]

For many of those who stayed behind in the city, there was no time to pick up the telephone to ask for help. This happened to a man named Andre who had decided to ride out the storm with his wife and young child in their two-story brick house in Gentilly. He allowed that it was his "fault" that they had stayed behind, thinking they would be safe in their sturdy home. But then "the water started coming so fast we had to scramble upstairs from the first floor.... That water came right behind us, waltzing up the stairs like it owned the place, and quick as a wink got to swirling around our ankles." Andre and his family were now marooned on their second floor. The water kept rising, and he was "thinking it would never stop," although it did finally top out around his waist. He, his wife, and their child stood their ground there, hoping that emergency personnel would soon arrive. As that dark and historic day gave way to an even darker night, he recalled the scene in vivid detail:

> About midnight, it was, I waded out on to the upstairs balcony from our bedroom to get a look. The water was running by my house just below the balcony railings, and I could see this black, oily surface going all around the block, filling streets and yards. People was yelling, banging on the roofs of houses from the inside. They'd climbed up to get away from the water and got themselves stuck in their attics with no way to break out. Two days earlier some politician had told everybody staying to make sure they had an axe in their house, especially in their attics. The news people, and the president even, had acted like the man was some sort of farm boy for saying such things. "Take your axes upstairs," he'd said, and those news folks had laughed. But here it was

a-flooding, and that nasty water was drowning folks like rats in their own houses, and you better know them folks wished now that they had them axes.[4]

Debbie Este was one of countless survivors who almost surely "wished now that they had them axes." Debbie, who was forty-seven years old when Katrina struck, had decided to ride out the storm with her two teenage daughters, Tiffany and Amanda, as well as her sixty-eight-year-old mother, Melissa. They lived together in a modest yellow, single-story house in the Lower Ninth Ward, which was also home to their three dogs, a cat, a guinea pig, a gerbil, six hamsters, and a parakeet. It must have been hard for Debbie, a former accountant who struggled with chronic pain and used a wheelchair to get around, to think of leaving home with all those pets, not to speak of her own ailments and her struggles to care for her children and aging mother. The family went to bed the night before Katrina made its appearance, uncertain of how bad the storm would be.

The next morning the Este family was jolted awake after the flood defenses near their house collapsed. The water flowed into their home, and within minutes it had become waist-deep. Tiffany, Debbie's oldest daughter, nearly drowned while trying to save her cat. "It started coming up, faster and faster," she said. At this point, Debbie realized, "we have to go in the attic, because that's the highest place I know of to go."

As the water rose, so too did the temperatures. It was 110 degrees in the attic, and they had no food and would soon run out of water. After a day and a half in those truly unbearable conditions, Debbie watched her own mother succumb to the heat. "We told her we loved her, and she said she loved us," Debbie said. "I told her I was sorry I couldn't help.…And she closed her eyes." The attic, meant to serve as a temporary refuge, was a deadly trap.

As Melissa, who suffered from congestive heart failure, now lay lifeless on the attic floor, Debbie and her daughters began to scream for help. They did so for hours, but without a way to break through their rooftop, their muffled calls went unanswered. As another day passed, Debbie grew increasingly distraught and began to consider using the painkillers she had with her to end her and her daughters' suffering. "I said, nobody's going to come save us up here and I don't want to die like this, three days laying in this stinky, dirty water.…We're going to die, why don't we just end it quicker?" Tiffany and Amanda pleaded with their mother, trying to keep a flicker of hope alive. Just when it seemed like all was lost, Debbie heard her brother's voice shouting her name. He had come to search for them in a boat, and he had brought an ax. As he chopped through the roof, more water poured in, raising the level in the attic. Six inches more, Debbie recalled later, "and we would have been dead."[5]

Experiencing a sense of life threat during a disaster has been defined elsewhere as "the feeling that one's life is in danger as an incident unfolds."[6] If a social scientist looking for "yes" or "no" answers to a questionnaire were to ask Debbie whether she "felt that her life was in danger in Hurricane Katrina," she would have either said "yes" or stared at the inquirer in speechless anguish. No single-syllable answer to that hypothetical question can even begin to capture the heartbreak of watching your own mother die, nor is there an indicator that incorporates the sense of utter hopelessness that would lead a mother to consider encouraging her daughters to take their own lives. There is important knowledge to be gained through counting the number of exposures that people experience in a disaster, but there are also risks that other forms of suffering may be overlooked—the batterings that eventually cover people like a heavy blanket, threatening to smother them at any moment.

Daniel Weber, a fifty-three-year-old lifelong New Orleans resident, heard the Industrial Canal levee fail. The breach inundated his neighborhood and flooded his home. Daniel's wife of twenty-three years, Rosetta, was wheelchair-bound after suffering a series of strokes. He could not move her into the attic, so he broke out a window and tried to push her out through the rising waters and then onto the roof. "I was pushing her up," Weber said, "and it got real quiet. I said, 'What's wrong baby?' She said, 'I'm saying my prayers.' I got real scared. That's when I grabbed her by her shirt. But the water took her away.... I jumped in after her but couldn't find her. I know she's probably dead. I wanted to die right then. I wanted to see God, stand there, and tell him, 'Look what you did to me?' If I could die tomorrow, I'd get right in his face and ask him 'What did you do?' "[7]

Daniel spent the next fourteen hours in water over his head, struggling to stay alive by clinging to tree branches and floating debris. Rescue workers eventually found him, lifted him from the waters, and ferried him to dry ground. But the memory of his wife offering a final prayer and then letting go of his hand is certain to have left a deep and everlasting wound.

When Daniel and so many others were taken to higher ground, they joined scores of people who had been left without basic life-sustaining essentials and, far worse, who had little indication that fellow humans from the outside world cared about the conditions they were enduring. By this time, many thousands had been drawn to the Convention Center or the

Superdome, seeking sanctuary from murky waters and the stifling heat. But understaffed and without sufficient supplies, the shelters of last resort became more like sweltering and surreal vaults. "We're just a bunch of rats," said one of the survivors caught up in a throng outside the Superdome. "That's how they've been treating us."[8]

The old and the sick who had somehow survived the killer winds and navigated the putrid floodwaters were now dying from the heat, the shortage of potable water, and the lack of proper medical care. Five days after Katrina made landfall, a man named Donyell said, "We're being treated like animals. Look around...look at the bodies. And there's no way for us to leave....It's not right. We're humans, too."[9]

Meanwhile, thousands more people were gathered on a highway overpass on Interstate 10, waiting for buses to take them away from a storm they had not been able to escape. A team of reporters described the scene there:

> Babies cried. The sick huddled in the shade in wheelchairs or rested on cots. Dawn Ray, 40, was in tears, looking after an autistic niece who had soiled herself and her son who is blind and has cerebral palsy. A few others, less patient, simply started walking west with nowhere to go, like a man pushing a bike in one hand and pulling a shopping cart in another.... "Disease, germs," one woman said, covering her mouth with a cloth, her voice smoldering with anger. "We need help. We don't live like this in America."[10]

That same team of journalists, writing from a different vantage point, tried to capture what happened after rescuers released the rescued on another elevated section of Interstate 10:

> Barefoot women cradling naked, screaming babies limped from a National Guard rescue truck, everything they owned on their backs after 36 hours of watching the floodwaters breach their doors, topple their refrigerators, and drive them to the only high ground available—roofs, trees, attics, and bridge spans. Behind them, elderly couples in nightgowns and slippers leaned on each other for support as they walked slowly from the helicopter that rescued them. Many clutched garbage bags holding all the possessions they could salvage; many had no more than damp tank tops and shorts clinging to their bodies. Most were hungry, thirsty, and alone.

Chermaine Daniels, 49, had left her flooded one-story house in the Ninth Ward on Tuesday morning, gashing her ankle on a fence as she struggled to swim to a neighbor's two-story house. Later that day, Ms. Daniels and several others were rescued by a uniformed officer in a boat and deposited at an I-10 encampment. "What do we do now?" she asked the boat driver. "You're on your own," the driver replied.[11]

This sense of being "on your own" pushed some to a breaking point. In a dramatic nationally televised appearance, Aaron Broussard, president of Jefferson Parish, which borders Orleans Parish to the south, began sobbing uncontrollably. He recounted a story of a local emergency management official receiving phone calls from his mother, who, trapped in a nursing home, pleaded day after day for rescue. Assured by federal officials, the man promised her repeatedly that help was on the way. Broussard, visibly choking back tears, described what happened:

> Every day she called him and said, "Are you coming, son? Is some-body coming?" And he said, "Yeah, mama, somebody's coming to get you." Somebody's coming to get you on Tuesday. Somebody's coming to get you on Wednesday. Somebody's coming to get you on Thursday. Somebody's coming to get you on Friday. And she drowned Friday night. She drowned Friday night.[12]

Broussard angrily denounced federal leadership and the anemic response efforts. "We have been abandoned by our own country," he said. "It's not just Katrina that caused all these deaths in New Orleans here. Bureaucracy has committed murder here in the greater New Orleans area, and bureaucracy has to stand trial before Congress now."[13]

Across the city, able-bodied children and adults stood for days on end on rooftops in the blazing hot August sun, waving white shirts and bedsheets like flags of surrender. They were trying to attract the attention of the search-and-rescue parties that they had heard were coming, and they were easily visible to the helicopters that were hovering about. Some of those helicopters were part of the airborne news media reporting on the situation on the ground. As they pointed their cameras on the scene below, they ensured that everyone in the country—in the world for that matter—could get a sense of what was going on down there.

It is easy to forget but worth remembering that Katrina was one of the first major disasters to be broadcast live on television. Once the media were in full stride in New Orleans after Katrina made its first appearance, journalists were clearing their throats and readying their cameras for what was ahead. It was obvious even then that race and poverty were playing a crucial role in that damaged social landscape, and the avalanche of published work that followed since has made that point very clearly.

The sight of the wholesale neglect of an already disadvantaged people was caught in the bright glare of television screens and color photos splashed across digital media. It would be a while before those broadcasters and most of the audience that had tuned in would absorb the full meaning of those unrelenting scenes, but the evidence was unmistakable. The suffering was on full display.

Those thick crowds of people gathered outside the Superdome in the fierce sunlight were waiting for help in a space that could be measured by the acre as well as the square yard. Michael Eric Dyson, a widely known expert on race and social life, later wrote, "Many colors were present in this multicultural stew of suffering, but the dominant color was black."[14]

FIGURE 6.1. Katrina survivors stretch as far as the eye can see in front of the Superdome. Photo © Charlie Varley, varleypix.com, 2005.

FIGURE 6.2. New Orleans residents seek higher ground.
Photo © Charlie Varley, varleypix.com, 2005.

The photographer Charlie Varley captured an image of a tight knot of people caught on what looks like a tiny island out in the middle of a murky lake. That clump of land rises no more than a foot or so above the level of the water surrounding it. Given a moment to consider, it becomes obvious that the visible parcel of ground is in fact the crest of a slight rise—all that is left of a landscape now covered with floodwaters. How many people are gathered there? Hundreds? They are waiting for a passing watercraft of some kind to take them to higher ground. The image gives new meaning to the word "stranded."

We turn now to a scene that was not captured by a camera but was witnessed by careful observers and then passed on to the public. We have already learned what those journalists saw when they visited the thousands of people who had found their way to the higher ground provided by roadway overpasses and bridges and other surfaces curving upward to accommodate automobile travel. The eye of the camera cannot tell us with any precision what the racial composition of those tight clusters of people were, but it is almost a certainty that the vast majority of them were African American. It was they, after all, who were left behind when evacuation orders sent most of the city's White residents—equipped with working automobiles and credit cards and other sources of support—out into safer locations. That these were mostly Black survivors seeking refuge atop infrastructure not intended for human occupation gives stark emphasis to the anguished comment of that team of visiting journalists, a rare lament for those professionals charged with reporting the news: "But most just waited with resigned patience—sad, angry, incredulous, scared, exhausted, people who seemed as discarded as the bottles of water and food containers that littered the ground."[15]

WHAT THE DATA CAN TELL US

One difficulty in trying to fully understand the character of racial inequality and how it shapes the nature of disaster in places like New Orleans is that the data we have on hand to describe its actual dimensions are so abstract, so detached, that they tell us almost nothing about the impact on the human spirit. We cite totals, percentages, averages, and the like, and we display those figures in equally abstract charts and graphs and tables. That is how researchers of all specialties gather information and then record their findings so that they can become a lasting contribution to knowledge.

Michael Eric Dyson concludes that "the most glaring feature" of the African Americans who were caught in the thrust of Katrina was that they were products of "concentrated poverty." They "lived in poor neighborhoods, attended poor schools, and had poorly paying jobs that reflected and reinforced a distressing pattern of rigid segregation."[16]

Dyson drew on mounds of available data to come to that conclusion. At the time of Katrina, as previously noted, 28 percent of the population of New Orleans lived in poverty, and 84 percent of those persons were African American. Those differences in wealth, in turn, influenced vast disparities in health. Mortality rates for African American infants in New Orleans were more than two times greater than for White infants. The life expectancy of African Americans living in some of the poorer neighborhoods in New Orleans was twenty to twenty-five years shorter than for Whites living in some of the wealthier parts of the city.[17] Numbers like those could splash across page after page. Among the many reasons data like these are essential is that they allow researchers and policymakers to measure and monitor racial and economic inequality.[18] But they tell us almost nothing about what often matters most about the lacerating pain of racism and poverty: the cruelty of it and the anxiety and depression that it can generate.

One of the benefits of the kind of research we are speaking of here—*watching* what is happening out in the real world and *listening to* what those who live there and experience it firsthand have to say about it—is the reminder that the suffering and moments of deep self-doubt we learn about in this way are rarely reflected in percentages and other measures. When a housekeeper notes that "my heart sinks every morning when I realize that I cannot provide my kids with a nourishing breakfast," she is not only touching a different emotional chord but offering a different category of data altogether.

When we look out over that urban scene with these issues in mind, what should we conclude about New Orleans in the time of Katrina? Most longtime residents, whether Black or White, well-off or barely making it, are likely to say without a moment's hesitation that racial inequality has been an obvious signature of the Crescent City since the beginning. Some lament that. Others ignore it, deny it, or even justify it, sometimes in public places but more often in the protection of private conversation. When Katrina swept across the city, however, that feature of the local culture—the outright neglect of Blackness for the benefit of Whiteness—was painfully obvious, not only across this country but across the world.

Any number of topics are worth pondering when discussion turns to those "laments" about racial inequality. We will draw attention to one in particular as we bring this section to a close. The African Americans of New Orleans, almost to a person, felt abandoned, not only by state and national agencies but by their fellow human beings, their fellow citizens, and their fellow townspeople. They felt as though they had been left behind to die. That was not a new feeling for them by any means. Their disappointment and anguish had been expressed long before. But that realization was sharply reinforced in this new time of crisis when some degree of camaraderie and neighborliness, however grudgingly offered, could have made a real difference.

That leaves one question hovering in the air: How well would this portrait of one very important urban setting serve as a portrait of the American social landscape more generally?

Social scientists and other students of the human scene tend to call the kinds of suffering that happened in Katrina by their old Greek name—*trauma* in the singular, *traumata*, or simply *traumas*, in the plural. "Trauma" is best translated from the original Greek as "wound." When sociologists use the term "trauma," as we do here, we are usually referring to an injury induced by a blow to the body or the mind. But the term "trauma" can be a good deal more ambiguous in other English usages, where it can refer to *either* the event that causes an injury or the injury that follows from it. Trauma, then, can mean the gunshot that struck human flesh or the wound caused by it. These two traumas occur simultaneously in the same split second in time, but within a very important difference in realities.

If we turn to dictionary definitions to resolve this ambiguity, we get very little assistance. The *Oxford English Dictionary* defines "trauma" both as "a deeply distressing or disturbing experience" and as an "emotional shock following a stressful event." The *Random House Dictionary* defines "trauma" as "an injury" and then as "a startling experience that has a lasting effect on mental life."

The term "trauma" can also be ambiguous in medical settings, where it sometimes means "an experience that produces psychological injury" but other times means "the injury so caused." But there is no ambiguity at all in most psychiatric and clinical psychological circles: in "post-traumatic stress disorder," "trauma" refers only to the event, the irritant, that resulted in an injury—the robbery, the collision, the earthquake rumbling up from below, the hurricane charging inland—and "stress" refers to the resulting injury—the disorientation, depression, or even death. The wound, in short.

We might well wonder whether "stress" is too mild a term for psychological damages like those caused by the terrors and butcheries of Auschwitz. If we think of a bad day at the office as "stressful," how meaningful is it to use that same term to speak of the feelings of human beings who have been victims of the worst horrors that life on earth can inflict? Can the experiences of the survivors of a genocide reasonably be placed on the same continuum as the experiences of those who are having a bad day, a rough week, or a difficult year? Is it useful to describe the loss of a child as "stressful"?

The main point here is that "trauma" makes sense in the social sciences only if it refers to the *injury* rather than to its *cause*. And we should add that terms like "blow" have a sharp, immediate sound to them, as if trauma can best be understood as a sudden jolt to the nervous system that leaves a lasting pain behind. A storm coming over the horizon and slamming into human settlements that are ill prepared for it, as happened when Katrina made landfall, would be a case in point.

Traumatic wounds can also result, however, from the accumulation over time of less dramatic assaults on the self—repeated slaps of fate can add up to a deep and lasting injury. Continuing exposure to moments of combat in warfare is an obvious example, but there are more subtle versions of trauma that cut just as deep: being continually exposed to abuse as a child, experiencing ongoing deprivations, living precariously for a long time on the edge of danger, or repeatedly enduring disrespect if not outright contempt from other human beings in one's environment. Those accumulating slaps can last a lifetime and permanently wound the spirit.

This type of experience can result in what one of us, Kai Erikson, called "the traumatic worldview" in an earlier publication.[19] Such a worldview can develop when the continuous pounding of traumatic happenings drives one into an entirely different frame of mind, a new way of conceptualizing reality—almost a new cultural ethos conceptually independent of its status as a psychiatric disorder. Traumatized people sometimes come to see the world differently, to calculate life's chances differently, to view the future differently. The "shock," that is to say, takes the form of new insights into the way things really are, a feeling that the world, and particularly its human element, is unreliable, unsteady, and dangerous and must be eyed warily.

What the rest of us need to acknowledge is that such views cannot be dismissed as delusions resulting from mental disarrangement. A good deal of the data flowing into our lives can logically support that very conclusion—that natural forces cannot always be relied on and that human social arrangements cannot always be trusted. One Holocaust veteran, speaking of the outlook he shared with his fellow survivors, put it exactly: "It's a view of the world, a total world view...of really knowing the truth about people, human nature, about death—of really knowing the truth in ways other people do not."[20]

Whether or not that frame of mind is seen from a psychiatric perspective as only a mental disorder, it can be viewed differently from a social science perspective. People who have lived through such difficult times have experienced things that most of the rest of us never have, and in that sense they can be seen as the true experts in that department of life. If they are suffering as a result, then of course they need to be offered clinical attention so that they can hope to be restored. But we should be listening to them attentively in the meantime and learning what we can from them, because persons who have had traumatic experiences view reality in a way that human cultures tend to shield us from. That is what the Holocaust survivor was saying: His eyes and those of his fellow sufferers were sharpened by agony. They can see realities that the rest of us cannot. Those visions should not be dismissed as illusions.

This leaves open another intriguing question, one which we will once again pose and then leave floating in midair. Survivors of disasters like Katrina share in common with the Holocaust survivor just quoted here a sense of knowing a truth that the rest of us do not. How much sense would it make for the rest of us to take advantage of that dark insight and put those survivors to work counseling newcomers to that realization? This type of counseling would almost certainly be of support to newcomers to trauma, and it might very well help the veterans of trauma find a place in the larger social order.

AFTER

THE PAINS OF DISPLACEMENT

Katrina was responsible for driving somewhere between one million and one and a half million people away from their homes.[1] This was not the largest mass evacuation on record. As many as two and a half million people have been known to flee along public highways to avoid incoming storms in Florida. But those evacuations were of relatively short duration. The evacuations caused by Katrina (and its cruel successor, Rita) were certain to be either longer term (for those who managed to return home) or permanent (for those who never did). The departure of New Orleans residents from their city after Katrina became a *diaspora*.

It is hard to find a comparison in this country. One possibility is the exodus from the Dust Bowl in the 1930s; as many as two and a half million people were caught in the undertow of unrelenting dust storms.[2] Another is the Great Migration—the flow of perhaps as many as six million people, most of them Black, from the rural South to the industrial North throughout the first half of the twentieth century.[3]

But Katrina was far and away the most *abrupt* mass dislocation in the United States in modern times. The migration from the Dust Bowl in the Midwest to the far western states took place over months, stretching into years. The migration of African Americans from southern states to the North took place over years, stretching into decades. But the evacuation of the territories affected by Katrina took place in a matter of hours, stretching into days.

Those who participated in those earlier migrations were evacuees in the sense that they were retreating from a threatened place and had little choice about leaving. The land and the associated local and regional economies could no longer sustain them, and so they were seeking a better life elsewhere.[4] But they usually had time to think about it, to plan, to pack, to choose their moment and even their destination.

It is also worth noting that migrants tend to flow along well-established creek beds. The place of landing was chosen for most of them beforehand by advance scouts, as were the pathways to be used to reach it. People who migrated from the Great Plains to California, or from the rural South to the cities of Chicago, Pittsburgh, and Cleveland, were following a course that had already been charted by pioneering family members and friends. Thus, many who chose to follow already established trails had kinfolk ready to welcome them upon their arrival and to help them settle.

In contrast, the human cells ejected from the living organism of their community in the Gulf region were blown by errant winds to every point of the compass. Some found shelter in faraway places like Albany, Anchorage, Denver, Minneapolis, Salt Lake City, and Las Vegas. One does not need to be wholly familiar with the civic culture of New Orleans to appreciate that these were strange and remote terrains to the city's evacuees. Most of them were not blown so far away. Roughly 40 percent landed, at least initially, in nearby parts of Louisiana, and another 40 percent landed in the surrounding states of Texas, Mississippi, Alabama, and Georgia, no more than a day's drive by car or bus from what had recently been their home address.[5] But for many of them, "home" remained as distant a reality as it was for those who found themselves thousands of miles away.

Many of those who ended up far from home after Katrina did not choose their destination. In the chaotic days after the storm, officials placed Katrina survivors in vehicles of every kind to move them out of the drowned city.[6] An untold number of these persons who were shuffled onto airplanes were informed of their destination before boarding and then told in midflight that they were heading somewhere else. This happened to quite a number of the estimated fifteen thousand Katrina survivors who ended up in Denver and surrounding regions in Colorado. They thought that they were on their way to Texas, only to find out that they had been rerouted to the Mile High City instead. Among that group destined for Denver was a forty-one-year-old African American man who described the terror and uncertainty that followed Katrina:

> I thought I was really going to die because me and my girls slept on the streets for five days. I didn't know where I was going. I just got on a plane. I was scared because I had never been on a plane before. Everybody thought they were going to San Antonio, but then they wind up here.[7]

One of the mothers who landed in Denver after Katrina spoke of another problem she had encountered at the New Orleans airport. She had

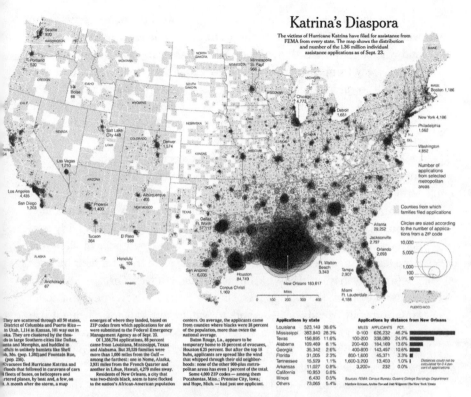

FIGURE 7.1. Map of the Katrina diaspora. Source: Matthew Ericson, Archie Tse, and Jodi Wilgoren, "Katrina's Diaspora," *New York Times,* October 2, 2005.

watched families being split apart there, and she refused to board any airplane until there were enough seats available for her and her children:

> Then there were planes leaving and I told them that I had five children, and I don't want to be separated. I told them I will not be separated from my kids because there were people crying, mothers crying saying that their kids are missing. So this one plane was about to take off and they needed three or four more people and I was like, "No, no, we need six seats." So we missed that plane and we waited for another couple of hours until the next plane could leave.[8]

This woman's decision to wait for the next flight probably spared her family the suffering of separation that more than five thousand children and their loved ones endured after Katrina.[9]

In an earlier chapter in this book, we described the busy rescuers who were in no position to pay attention to groups needing to stay together and who spread them all over the nation in their need to fill one bus and send it away from the curb so that they could begin loading another. It is not hard to understand the frantic urgency of those moments, but it *is* hard to understand why the agencies that put those processes into motion had so little appreciation for the desperation of the individuals they were rescuing and their need to remain together. This is why Jane Henrici once described the governmental agents who were supposed to be in charge of the evacuation as skilled in "the systematic practice of dividing and scattering families."[10]

Many evacuees who were separated from their family and then landed in those far-flung places would soon learn that they were in a fairly precarious position. Many of them, split apart from loved ones in ways that were largely inconceivable prior to the storm, were truly on their own for the first time in their lives. One former resident of New Orleans gave voice to just how stark the change was: "Before Katrina...you knew you could count on your friends or neighbors to watch your kids for a while if you needed to get out of the house. I didn't need to worry if I wanted to get out of the house because I could always call their father and he would come over for a little while. Here, there is just *no one* around to help."[11] Another lifelong resident of the city who was displaced far away after the storm said: "Before Katrina, if I needed a babysitter, I did not need to worry. I would just bring her [young daughter] around the corner at any given time. It is always knowing that somebody is right there.... But here you do not have that. You do not have any support whatsoever."[12]

The evacuees' sense of being unsupported and unmoored was reinforced by the view among a large share of the communities where survivors found refuge that they were offering staging areas and temporary shelters, not long-term resettlement. Their welcome, though warm and generous and heartening, often turned out to be short-term. A social worker in one of the communities that received large numbers of Katrina evacuees summed up the shift in the response:

Here is how I've seen people reacting more recently. "You aren't my neighbor. You aren't family. You weren't even in my state, and you're coming in here." Okay? At first it was "Oh, poor you!" But then after a while it became, "You're not going to go away, and I've got to pick up the cost."[13]

Another social worker suggested that "Katrina fatigue" was a "significant issue" that had seriously diminished the hurricane survivors' prospects for successful resettlement. She observed that there was something dramatically different about this disaster; rooted in the widespread displacement, it affected the entire recovery process:

> In Katrina, what is especially challenging is the disaster started in one place and it's ending in another place. This is a complete anomaly in disasters, because most disasters start and end in one place. In the normal case, the entire community will be affected. Thus their empathy doesn't end, because you were my neighbor beforehand, and my God, this horrible thing happened, so I'm going to help you out until you're back on your feet, because I knew you before and now I'm watching you struggle and I want to help you get back to where you were previously. But with Katrina ending in a new place, it's bizarre, because people aren't connected in the same way.... So I think on a community level, what I've seen a lot of is: "Isn't that over yet?" "Haven't you moved on?" "Do you have a job?"[14]

Already confronted with an uphill climb, tens of thousands of evacuees endured additional relocations and uncertainties in the months and years following Katrina.[15] It was not all that unusual for people to experience ten or twelve moves as they circled like birds in search of a place to land. For many, drifting around this way became a form of chronic dislocation.

The terms used to describe this scattering of people soon shifted from "evacuees," which means persons removed temporarily from a place of danger, to "migrants," meaning persons who move from one place to another either permanently or for long periods of time. It did not take long for "exiles" to work its way into that vocabulary as well, because it was becoming increasingly clear, as we have emphasized through this account, that the persons in charge of that piece of land known as "New Orleans" on the official map simply did not want the city's evacuees to return. Ever.

"Displaced" is a term widely used to refer to individuals who have become separated from their roots, their native place. That can be a fairly vague concept spatially. It can mean a particular tract of land, a village, a neighborhood, a parish, a commune, and so on. Displacement in that spatial context means being torn from the place where one belongs, is a natural part of, is attached to. But it can also mean something quite different. Many people in modern times find themselves in situations where they have not moved an inch from their original location on the land but have come to feel homeless nonetheless because the ground underneath them and the landscape surrounding them no longer have the feel of familiar terrain. "Rooted" means being connected to a particular place and drawing nourishment from it. To become "uprooted," in that more abstract sense, is to be torn from the land because one no longer feels attached to it or nourished by it. One woman, twenty-eight years old when Katrina roared ashore, described her loss of a sense of place and a sense of community even though she remains in her original homeland: "I don't know where my family is...I done lost everything. My high school—gone. My elementary school—gone. I can't even bring my kids and show them where I come from." "Displaced" is the right word to describe that feeling of disconnectedness.

Those caught up in the mass displacement that followed Katrina either knew or soon learned that they were not regarded as worthy neighbors by those with whom they had once shared a city, and they wondered if they were even regarded as fully human by these fellow residents. They were not wanted in the only place where they felt at home and, for many, the only place they had ever called home.

We cannot be sure of how this particular dynamic shaped the resettlement patterns of New Orleanians, but what is clear is that the city is now Whiter and has a smaller human footprint than before the storm. The city is home to some ninety thousand fewer souls than before Katrina. Unsurprisingly, the Black population has borne the brunt of the displacement. The Black middle and upper classes are significantly reduced, leaving a remaining Black population that is poorer overall. In 2013, for example, the median Black household income in New Orleans was just over $25,000; adjusted for inflation, that is $5,000 *less* than the median income in the year 2000.[16]

For those former residents who wished to return to New Orleans but could not find a way, the suffering could be almost palpable. Several years after Katrina, one of us met an elderly African American man named James who was among those who had been placed on one of those airplanes believed to be routed to Texas that ended up in Denver. He said several times that he "could not breathe" after he arrived in the city, which is located 5,280 feet above sea level. One might think at first that the elevation was too high and the air too thin and dry for his aging lungs. But as he continued to share his overwhelmingly sad tale of separation from family and home, it became obvious that his difficulties had very little if anything to do with the altitude. He was trying to describe the sense of suffocation that can result from social isolation. James felt "trapped and alone" in what was a wholly unfamiliar location. And he knew what would cure his breathing issues. "I have to go home," he said. "If I could just get back to New Orleans, that is where I can breathe again."

James was alone and adrift. He had been sent to a destination not of his choosing, with few social supports. This was a common experience for thousands of evacuees.[17] And for a striking number of them, finding a place for a displaced family to land became the responsibility of the women household keepers in the family—the "networkers and caregivers," the "connective tissue of the family and of the community," as Carol Bebelle, a prominent civic leader in New Orleans, called them.[18]

As noted in chapter 5, Katherine Browne documented the experiences of a family so large that it stretched the very meaning of "extended" onto an entirely new plane. A member of that family had moved to Dallas prior to Katrina with her husband. She arranged for well over a hundred people in her family to use her large two-story home as a sort of evacuation headquarters where family members could gather, cook, reminisce, and strategize for the long recovery ahead.[19]

Jacquelyn Litt wrote of a family of fifty-four members who left New Orleans together in what she described as an "evacuation chain."[20] They made their way to a two-bedroom duplex in Baton Rouge where they all stayed for six weeks. The key person in making that arrangement—the "network anchor"—was a woman named Miss Joanne. She and her husband owned the duplex and insisted on sleeping in the hallway themselves for the convenience of their guests.

In her research after Katrina, Elizabeth Fussell chronicled the trajectory of evacuees who took refuge in narrow spaces for what must have seemed like long spans of time: an apartment that contained fifteen guests at the beginning and grew in number as the evacuation continued; another two-bedroom apartment with seventeen guests; and yet another with twenty-seven. Fussell describes this kind of situation: "Whether they evacuated before or after the hurricane struck, nearly all of the women explained their preparations for the hurricane as a social network–based strategy with the goal of remaining together while coping with the hurricane's effects."[21]

It became clear as federal and state agencies began their awkward efforts to try to help the most badly harmed people exposed to Katrina that they did not speak the same language as their clients, they looked at the world in different ways, and they came from quite different social orbits. They were strangers when they faced one another in office settings, strangers when they tried to talk with one another over the telephone. For example, one of the many voices that the sociologists Steve Kroll-Smith, Vern Baxter, and Pam Jenkins learned so much from after Katrina was that of a young woman who hung up after a very frustrating phone conversation with a FEMA agent and said to the person visiting her: "Sweet Jesus, what planet is she from?"[22] It was as if the world she was trying to enter looked to the agent like a foreign territory. She spoke a different language, surveyed a different human scene, and in that sense was not really there at all. After listening to hundreds of similar comments, these authors concluded: "The work of the public sector to provide needed relief and assistance" was "itself a source of profound disorder and confusion, a kind of second disaster."[23] In the end, they raised a critical query: "How does one recover from 'recovery'?"[24]

In her book *Standing in the Need*, Katherine Browne writes of the "wilderness" that separated "deeply wounded" families from the "alien cultures of the Federal Emergency Management Agency, the Red Cross, middle-class churches, and landlords."[25] After recounting a particularly painful moment when one of the women at the center of the family could not get assistance from FEMA with her long-pending housing application, Browne observes: "No official seemed to understand the unusual size of [the] family group," nor did anyone realize that to recover from the disaster, the family had to be treated as a collective.[26] Browne adds that one of the benefits made available was mental health counseling in the form of office visits with a trained psychotherapist. But that made no sense at all to these sufferers. "People managed trouble together," Browne points out.[27] What good could come from a single visit to a single counselor in a sealed-off office? It was a group problem, not an individual one.[28]

Agents of FEMA and other agencies that came to town from the outside intending to help those who had been caught up in the furor saw what we have been calling the "nuclear family" as the true definition of family. As had happened during the evacuation period, this definition underpinned the thoughts and actions of most agents who were ostensibly there to assist over the long term. For example, they operated on the assumption that every family unit had the ability and the means to leave town when required to—a problem we discussed earlier—as well as the flexibility to find safe places to land while in transit. The temporary shelters available to the newly homeless after Katrina were cramped trailers, hotel rooms, or vacant apartments, all clearly designed for smaller family units, and that turned out to be a serious problem for many survivors. Checks were made out to the imagined head of household, most often a man, rather than to the person who was functioning in that role, most often a woman.

One might not place blame on individual FEMA staff members or representatives of other government-backed programs. They were either carrying out official policies or doing the best they could in the absence of instructions. But the agencies they worked for should at least have recognized and taken into account the differences in the family structures of those they had been sent to assist. In the end, by failing to do so, they were massively insensitive to this critical disconnect between what, after all, are different cultural forms within the same national entity. To ignore that divide is to take the risk of imposing suffering rather than providing relief and of badly underestimating the actual human toll of the disaster.

As the title of this book indicates, Katrina has to be seen as a continuing event. The disaster upended countless lives, and it still rages as an inner storm with no end for many who escaped the winds and waters but have not escaped the traumatic injuries that ensued. As we bring this chapter to a close, more than fifteen years have passed since Katrina first landed on the Louisiana Gulf Coast. A considerable number of the younger survivors are now parents themselves. Will the sufferings of the storm be passed on in some form to their children? Will these younger Katrina survivors be better prepared for that inevitable next time always lurking around the corner?

We cannot know the answers to these questions, but we ask them with a growing sense of urgency. As climate change accelerates and social inequality worsens, there will be more disasters like Katrina. We look back to that storm and its aftermath in the hope that, as we move forward and rebuild, we can not only learn from those survivors but also honor them, keeping the insights they have passed on to us in mind.

POSTLUDE

We live in an age when the flow of everyday life is interrupted more and more often by disasters of one kind or another. They dominate our attention for a time, eliciting both a riveting sense of horror and a deep sense of compassion. After a while, they drift out of our immediate line of vision as other matters take their turn on the surface of our mind. The horrors do not disappear from memory, of course. They shift into other compartments of thought reserved for things past.

Quite a number of catastrophes have occurred around the world in the years since we launched the Katrina Bookshelf, an effort to explore the human costs of disaster. A small but significant share of those events have far exceeded Katrina in terms of the number of lives lost or the economic and environmental damage wrought. The global Covid-19 pandemic stands out most prominently in that regard, but many other events are worth solemnly remembering as well. As we suggested in the initial pages of this book, however, there are compelling reasons to keep Katrina in active focus, not least because deadlier and more disruptive extreme events continue to appear with increasing regularity. As we bring this book to a close, we offer three additional explanations for the importance of the long-term study of disaster.

First, Katrina revealed a large array of human troubles that preceded the hurricane's landfall, including: systemic racism and poverty; political corruption; residential segregation and collective abandonment of public institutions; and resource extraction and unchecked environmental degradation. These and so many other social ills were not caused by Katrina. They were the precursors to the immense suffering that followed in the storm's wake.

The reasonable impulse of many disaster researchers, regardless of discipline, is to focus on the immediate aftermath of an event. But the impacts that follow are only comprehensible when placed in the context of a much broader arc of time. Just as a medical doctor cannot fully understand the progression of a disease without taking into account a patient's preexisting conditions, researchers cannot explain why disaster losses are patterned in particular ways without tracing the history of affected people and places. Most social science projects launched after Katrina glanced briefly at a relatively small fragment of a much wider expanse of detail. These research glances were often designed and analyzed with every precision allowed by the methods of modern science, but they were snapshots of a larger whole. For that reason, their contribution to the overall picture becomes evident only when they are assembled, like the thousands of tesserae that together make up a mosaic.

Second, only when equipped with an informed understanding of disaster events are decision-makers in a position to make a full commitment to a just and reasoned restoration. As we noted earlier, "restoration" in this sense refers not simply to reconstruction of the physical infrastructure of the affected area but also to restoration of the persons who were harmed as a consequence of the storm.

As Katrina made apparent, that latter dimension of "restoration" has depended on discovering the whereabouts and the condition of the many thousands of evacuees who became part of one of the most wrenching diasporas in the history of the country. It has also been contingent on discovering how those who remained in place and tried to create new lives on the ruins of the old are now faring. Every indication we have from both short- and much longer-term studies of Katrina suggests that many of the survivors have been wounded emotionally or physically by the experience. This is particularly the case for African Americans, the poor, children, the elderly, and the infirm.

Third, the action needed to restore both the physical infrastructure and the lives of those who absorbed Katrina's severest blows cannot be engaged without scientific investigations of the type described here, but those investigations take time and resources. Moreover, the results are not always delivered in a way that allows decision-makers to decipher what needs to be done in the near term. This difficulty does not diminish the need for this kind of longitudinal work. Instead, it helps to make the case for why the information that was gathered in the wake of Katrina can and should continue to be used to help prepare the nation for hurricanes and other calamities.

When viewed through a social science lens, Katrina was virtually the perfect storm. It destroyed whole communities. It was responsible for an unprecedented rate of traumatic reactions among some of the most vulnerable population groups in this country. It led to one of the most disruptive dislocations on record. And it resulted in a number of severe issues for both the communities in the path of the storm and the communities that provided refuge to those who fled from it. In these respects, Katrina offered a grim preview of so many of the disasters that have followed it and for all that the future has in store. As a devastating case in point, on August 29, 2021—the sixteenth anniversary of Katrina's landfall—Hurricane Ida walloped the Gulf Coast with 150 mile-per-hour winds and lashing rainfall. Ida, which is now tied for the rank of the strongest hurricane on record in Louisiana, laid waste to coastal communities that had not yet recovered from Katrina or the many named storms that have done considerable damage in the years since. This reality only underscores the urgency of implementing lessons as they are learned.

In the opening pages of this book, we wrote that one of the most important objectives of sociologists is to describe events in such a way that they can serve as a *lens* through which other investigators can get a useful perspective. In that sense, Katrina has sharpened the focus of researchers, helping them to see more clearly the dimensions of other disasters unfolding in our midst. This is especially true of the Covid-19 pandemic, which as of this writing has claimed close to 900,000 lives here in the United States and more than 5.6 million globally. Although the virus—much like the hurricane that came almost two decades before it—was initially depicted as an equal opportunity threat, the lens so carefully refined in Katrina helped capable observers to question that narrative. Louisiana, interestingly, was the first state in the nation to release Covid-19 data by race. The statistics were as unsettling as they were unsurprising. While African Americans make up only one-third of the state's population, they initially accounted for 70 percent of deaths related to Covid-19.[1] Other states and counties soon followed Louisiana's lead, and as Katrina had done many years prior, the pandemic yet again stripped bare the racial divide in this nation. Study after study showed that Black Americans, Latinos, and Native Americans were getting sick, being hospitalized, and dying at disproportionate rates when compared to Whites.[2]

Why? The answers to that simple query were illuminated by lessons learned in Katrina. Perhaps the most notable lesson was that we can make sense of such gaping disparities only by looking at a constellation of social, economic, and historic factors that explain why people who have been relegated to the literal and figurative margins of society are the least prepared when trouble comes to visit. This is exactly what has happened in the pandemic. People of color are more likely to live in households whose adults have been deemed essential workers and are therefore more likely to be exposed to the virus and to bring it home from the workplace. Also, the more crowded conditions in which they often live make it difficult, if not impossible, to take recommended protective actions. Communities of color bear a disproportionate burden of the nation's pollution, and those who reside in contaminated places almost always have less access to health care, healthful food, and open spaces. These and so many other factors cluster together and help explain why those at the margins have been so much more likely to get sick and die during the pandemic.

Another way that a perspective formed in the past has been instructive during this time of pandemic is less obvious but no less important. Katrina led to the most abrupt large-scale displacement in our national history, while the onset of Covid-19 resulted in widespread orders to shelter in place. In both cases, however, large family groupings have borne a special burden. This happened in Katrina because such extended family units were so often separated from one another during the displacement. In the pandemic, the gathering of families, often in tight spaces, was exactly what left them exposed and at risk of catching the deadly virus.

Taking an even broader view, Katrina and Covid-19 also share what one of the present authors once called "collective trauma."[3] This form of trauma, which is expressed through the loss of communality, takes the form of a feeling deep inside that one has been left alone on an empty plain without that inner circle of others—familial, neighborly, communal—on which our kind has relied from the beginning. What happened in Katrina, particularly in New Orleans, was a sudden re-sorting of the human landscape. Some persons were sent away altogether, while others remained exactly where they had always been—sometimes for generations—but looking out at a scene of frightening disorder. Without the sense of communal gathering, home no longer felt like home. During the pandemic, physicians and other specialists have been clear in their insistence that human beings would be much safer if they retreated into small family clusters. No sensible person can argue with that logic. But it is very important to keep in mind at the same time—this being one of the lessons of Katrina—that clustering of that kind can be very painful and even harmful for persons who see larger gatherings as the only natural kind of family constellation. This can place individuals in a vulnerable spot, a kind of double jeopardy. When they observe the rules of quarantine, they are far more likely to suffer from a deep sense of anguish resulting from the isolation. And when they are driven to venture out into places where extended families feel at home again, feel alive again—places of worship, playgrounds, village greens, street corners, backyards, and so on—they are at greater risk of exposure. The emotional toll has been high. The orders to stay apart undoubtedly saved many lives, but at what cost? That question will take more time to sort out.

* * *

Experts, for all practical purposes, are unanimous in predicting that in the coming decades, we will see a marked increase in the number and severity of catastrophic events resulting from the rampages of an ever more turbulent natural world, the miscalculations of an ever more incautious human world, the widening gap between the rich and the poor, and the particular distributions of a growing human population.

Knowing is far and away our surest line of defense against the harm done by future catastrophes, which will certainly involve damage to large population centers, massive dislocations of persons, and the infliction of physical and emotional wounds on vast numbers of people. Katrina offered a remarkable opportunity to learn at least a part of what the nation will need to know in order to be prepared for this future. May we take the lessons and apply them.

ACKNOWLEDGMENTS

The Katrina Bookshelf, of which this book is a part, was the result of a decade and a half of scholarly collaboration between the members of what would come to be called the Social Science Research Council Task Force on Hurricane Katrina.[1] In these closing pages, we share the names of many of the people who contributed to the research efforts described in this book and in the other books that sit on what we now refer to simply as "the Shelf."

The story of this effort opens at a meeting in New York that was convened a few weeks after Katrina's deadly landfall.[2] In attendance were Cynthia Fuchs Epstein, who was then the president of the American Sociological Association (ASA); Troy Duster, the immediate past ASA president; and Frances Fox Piven, the president-elect. Craig Calhoun, who was then the SSRC president, provided the meeting space and a welcoming intellectual home for the gatherings to follow. Those leaders invited Kai Erikson to spearhead the initiative that would grow into the SSRC Task Force and, much later, the Katrina Bookshelf. This may have been the first time that the senior officers of the ASA came together to encourage such an ambitious program of research on a singular event. It is an act that is worth remembering, applauding, and, we hope, repeating in the future.

The ASA had really started something, and the SSRC soon became our institutional home. With that home came the creation of the SSRC Task Force and a decision to commit ourselves to this effort for the long haul. The support of the broader SSRC staff was integral to the entire enterprise.

The Task Force initially involved a relatively small group of researchers who were veterans of the study of disaster. Over the years, that core expanded to include: Vernon Baxter, Katherine Browne, Lee "Chip" Clarke, Ronald Eyerman, Alice Fothergill, William Freudenburg, Elizabeth Fussell, Cynthia Garza, Robert Gramling, Pamela Jenkins, Shirley Laska, Laura Lein, Jacquelyn Litt, Rachel Luft, Brent Marshall, Beverly Mason, Lee Miller, Harvey Molotch, Jessica Pardee, John Steven Picou, and Lynn Weber. Steve Kroll-Smith served as coordinator of research projects, Lori Peek as associate chair, and Kai Erikson as chair. Many students and other early career researchers contributed mightily to the studies launched by the Task Force members. The work of these additional collaborators was instrumental in all that followed.[3]

The Task Force was soon collaborating with the Institute for Women's Policy Research (IWPR), under the leadership of Heidi Hartmann, the IWPR president and CEO. Jane Henrici and Avis Jones-DeWeever, both with IWPR then, attended several early meetings at the SSRC. Their insights helped sharpen the race, class, and gender analyses that appear in the pages of the books on the Shelf.

During the initial stages of the work, the Task Force was advised by a group of thoughtful and generous scholars. Advisory board members included: Susan Cutter, John Darley, Bonnie Thornton Dill, Nancy Foner, Heidi Hartmann, Ira Katznelson, Nicholas Lemann, Harvey Molotch, Katherine Newman, Kenneth Prewitt, Rubén Rumbaut, Kathleen Tierney, and Mary Waters.

As the research progressed, Task Force members began to share drafts of the manuscripts they were writing with other authors to assure that their work would fit into that larger whole. We, in turn, started searching for an academic press to publish the books that would eventually appear on the Shelf. In time, and after a warm introduction from Katherine Browne, we received a letter from the then-editor-in-chief of the University of Texas Press, Theresa May. A native Texan, she had also watched up close as the heartbreak of Katrina unfolded. As thousands of displaced survivors poured into Austin after the storm, she, like many other residents of the city, had stepped in to try to help. She was moved by the suffering of the evacuees but also by their strength, and she recognized the importance of capturing their stories, as this series offered to do. Soon enough, she met with several members of the Task Force during a conference in San Antonio and agreed to publish the series that would soon be called the Katrina Bookshelf.

Theresa retired midway through the publication process, but before she left the press, she assured us that she would soon pass the baton to the best hands possible. Her words turned out to be so true. Robert Devens has guided the formation of the Katrina Bookshelf with a wisdom that stretches beyond his years. We are, and will always remain, grateful for both Theresa and Robert and their abiding commitment to this series as a whole and to our book. Robert also secured thoughtful reviews from Eric Klinenberg and another anonymous reviewer for this book; we are indebted for the many helpful suggestions they provided. We also acknowledge Adrienne Gilg, Robert Kimzey, Gianna LaMorte, Joel Pinckney, and the other talented members of the team at the University of Texas Press who helped to finalize and launch this book.

In 2010, we hosted a meeting in New York at which several advisers to the project and close colleagues read earlier drafts of this and other manuscripts set to appear on the Katrina Bookshelf. We benefited enormously from the written and verbal comments provided by Elijah Anderson, Carol Bebelle, Andrew Beveridge, Patricia Hill Collins, Cynthia Fuchs Epstein, Mindy Thompson Fullilove, Heidi Hartmann, Ira Katznelson, Douglas Massey, Cecilia Menjívar, Frances Fox Piven, Bill Quigley, Carol Stack, Eric Wanner, Mary Waters, and William Julius Wilson.

We also want to thank our colleagues who read earlier drafts of the text and provided suggestions to strengthen what you now see in print. Those generous readers included Vern Baxter, Katherine Browne, Ronald Eyerman, Alice Fothergill, Pamela Jenkins, Steve Kroll-Smith, Shirley Laska, Jacquelyn Litt, Harvey Molotch, Keith Nicholls, John Ryden, Carol Stack, and Jennifer Tobin.

When we visited New Orleans and the Gulf Coast, we benefited from the local knowledge and warm welcome of many scholars and practitioners in the region. Allyson Plyer of the Data Center was a trusted source of information from the earliest days after Katrina and up to now. Andy Horowitz added a crucial historical perspective—first through his dissertation research and later in the pages of his book—from which we learned so much. Katy Reckdahl is a special journalist with a heart as strong as the words she places on the page. Carol Bebelle served as a moral anchor through the storm, as well as an intellectual force who helped us to find our way back on course. Bill Quigley became a special kind of colleague in this endeavor. His wisdom, insight, and sheer vigor are reflected throughout these pages because his writings and his person helped shape our way of thinking, our way of seeing, and even our way of feeling to such a degree.

Several former students at Colorado State University and the University of Colorado Boulder contributed in many ways to this book. As these budding scholars searched for obscure references and sorted through newspaper archives, they became nothing short of co-conspirators in this entire effort. We offer our enduring gratitude to Jessica Austin, Charles Beller, Erica Schelly Billingsley, Candace Evans, Michelle Meyer, Meghan Mordy, and Kamryn Roper-Fetter.

We gratefully acknowledge the financial support of the American Sociological Association, Russell Sage Foundation, MacArthur Foundation, Ford Foundation, Rockefeller Foundation, and Bill and Melinda Gates Foundation. Each organization contributed different amounts of funding to the Task Force, but they all shared a common vision for advancing the understanding of the human impacts and societal consequences of Katrina.

This final entry on the Katrina Bookshelf has been a long time in the making, and it would not have been possible without the support of people who care for us and various institutions that have sustained us. Kai would like to thank his wife, Joanna Erikson, as well as his two sons, Keith and Christopher. Lori would like to thank her husband, Povilas Jocas, and their son, Kedras.

We close now with a final few words about our collaboration. Each of us owes a special thanks to the other. Our paths have become a shared one for many years now, having met at one of the earliest gatherings of what became the Katrina Task Force. We brought varying competencies and experiences to our team, and that collaboration has continued without a pause for all that time. It gives new meaning to the word "colleagueship," and it was during one of our weekly morning meetings when the first seeds of this book were planted. Over the years, it was the people around us who helped cultivate the initial work and stood by us as it grew into something more than we had initially imagined. We want our collaborators to know how much they mean to us, and we hope that the disaster survivors everywhere know how much we care for them.

NOTES

PRELUDE

1. Lori Peek and Kai Erikson, "Hurricane Katrina," in *Blackwell Encyclopedia of Sociology*, 2nd ed., edited by George Ritzer and Chris Rojek, pp. 1–7, https://doi.org/10.1002/9781405165518.wbeosh063.pub2 (Oxford: Blackwell, 2017).
2. John L. Beven, Lixion A. Avila, Eric S. Blake, Daniel P. Brown, James L. Franklin, Richard D. Knabb, Richard J. Pasch, Jamie R. Rhome, and Stacy R. Stewart, "Atlantic Hurricane Season of 2005," *Monthly Weather Review* 136, no. 3 (2008): 1109–1173, p. 1140.
3. Richard D. Knabb, Jamie R. Rhome, and Daniel P. Brown, "Tropical Cyclone Report: Hurricane Katrina, 23–30 August 2005" (Miami: National Hurricane Center, 2005), p. 12.
4. Associated Press, "Hurricane Katrina Plows into Louisiana but Spares New Orleans Its Full Fury," *Deseret News*, August 29, 2005, https://www.deseret.com/2005/8/29/19909510/hurricane-katrina-plows-into-louisiana-but-spares-new-orleans-its-full-fury (accessed September 21, 2021).
5. Maya Bell and Sentinel Staff Writer, "Last-Minute Shift Spares New Orleans Worst of Katrina," *Orlando Sentinel*, August 30, 2005, https://www.orlandosentinel.com/news/os-xpm-2005-08-30-canetrack30-story.html (accessed December 11, 2021).
6. Joseph B. Treaster and Kate Zernike, "Hurricane Katrina Slams into Gulf Coast; Dozens Are Dead," *New York Times*, August 30, 2005, p. A-1.
7. Eric Klinenberg, *Heat Wave: A Social Autopsy of Disaster in Chicago*, 2nd ed. (Chicago: University of Chicago Press, 2015).
8. Steve Matthewman, *Disasters, Risks, and Revelation: Making Sense of Our Times* (London: Palgrave Macmillan, 2015).
9. Shirley Laska, Susan Howell, and Alessandra Jerolleman, "'Built-In' Structural Violence and Vulnerability: A Common Threat to Resilient Disaster Recovery," in *Creating Katrina, Rebuilding Resilience*, edited by Michael J. Zakour, Nancy B. Mock, and Paul Kadetz, pp. 99–129 (Amsterdam: Elsevier, 2018).
10. Lori Peek, "They Call It 'Katrina Fatigue': Displaced Families and Discrimination in Colorado," in *Displaced: Life in the Katrina Diaspora*, edited by Lynn Weber and Lori Peek, pp. 31–46 (Austin: University of Texas Press, 2012).
11. Kai Erikson, *A New Species of Trouble: The Human Experience of Modern Disasters* (New York: W. W. Norton & Co., 1994).

1. Marc Giudici, "Hurricane Katrina: The Ethical Responsibility of the Media in Their Coverage of the Recovery Process," *Media Psychology Review* 1, no. 1 (2008), p. 3.

2. Associated Press, "Bush: Response "Not Acceptable," *The Denver Post*, September 2, 2005, https://www.denverpost.com/2005/09/02/bush-response -not-acceptable/ (accessed November 29, 2021).

3. US Executive Office of the President, Assistant to the President for Homeland Security and Counterterrorism, *The Federal Response to Hurricane Katrina: Lessons Learned* (Washington, DC: US Government Printing Office, 2006), p. 34, https://georgewbush-whitehouse.archives.gov/reports/katrina-lessons -learned/index.html (accessed September 22, 2021).

4. Jan Moller, "Notes from a Plane Flight," *New Orleans Times-Picayune*, August 30, 2005.

5. Roy A. Bernardi, "Federal Housing Response to Hurricane Katrina," testimony before the Committee on Financial Services, U.S. House of Representatives, February 6, 2007 (Washington, DC: US Government Printing Office, 2007), p. 43, https://www.govinfo.gov/content/pkg/CHRG-110hhrg34671/html/CHRG -110hhrg34671.htm (accessed September 21, 2021).

6. William R. Freudenburg, Robert B. Gramling, Shirley Laska, and Kai Erikson, *Catastrophe in the Making: The Engineering of Katrina and the Disasters of Tomorrow* (Washington, DC: Island Press, 2009), p. 117.

7. John C. Pine, "Hurricane Katrina and Oil Spills: Impact on Coastal and Ocean Environments," *Oceanography* 19, no. 2 (2006): 37–39.

8. For more on that devastating disaster, see William R. Freudenburg and Robert Gramling, *Blowout in the Gulf: The BP Oil Spill Disaster and the Future of Energy in America* (Cambridge, MA: MIT Press, 2010).

9. US Executive Office of the President, *The Federal Response to Hurricane Katrina*, p. 8.

10. JoAnne DeRouen, George Wooddell, and Robert Gramling, "Going Home: Re-Creating Community," unpublished manuscript (2012).

11. Ibid.

12. Ibid.

13. Matthew Brown, "Despite Devastation, Plaquemines Parish Death Tally Holds at Three," *New Orleans Times-Picayune*, September 8, 2005.

14. S. Jeffress Williams, "Louisiana Coastal Wetlands: A Resource at Risk," US Geological Survey Fact Sheet (1995), https://pubs.usgs.gov/fs/la-wetlands (accessed July 23, 2019).

15. Ibid.

16. Personal email communication, September 3, 2005.

17. For the definitive account of the impact of Katrina on the Mississippi Gulf Coast, see Susan L. Cutter, Christopher T. Emrich, Jerry T. Mitchell, Walter

W. Piegorsch, Mark M. Smith, and Lynn Weber, *Hurricane Katrina and the Forgotten Coast of Mississippi* (Cambridge: Cambridge University Press, 2014).

18. Carrie E. Lasley, "Catastrophes and the Role of Social Networks in Recovery: A Case Study of St. Bernard Parish, LA, Residents after Hurricane Katrina," PhD diss., University of New Orleans, August 2, 2012, https://scholarworks .uno.edu/td/1504.

19. J. Steven Picou, "Katrina as a Natech Disaster: Toxic Contamination and Long-Term Risks for Residents of New Orleans," *Journal of Applied Social Science* 4 (2009): 39–55.

20. Fran H. Norris, Matthew J. Friedman, Patricia J. Watson, Christopher M. Byrne, Eolia Diaz, and Krzysztof Kaniasty, "60,000 Disaster Victims Speak: Part I. An Empirical Review of the Empirical Literature, 1981–2001," *Psychiatry: Interpersonal and Biological Processes* 65, no. 3 (2002): 207–239.

21. Courte C. W. Voorhees, John Vick, and Douglas D. Perkins, " 'Came Hell and High Water': The Intersection of Hurricane Katrina, the News Media, Race, and Poverty," *Journal of Community and Applied Social Psychology* 17, no. 6 (2007): 415–429.

CHAPTER 2: ON THE STREETS OF NEW ORLEANS

1. Gary Rivlin, *Katrina: After the Flood* (New York: Simon & Schuster, 2015).

2. Part of the problem, as Bernie Cook suggests in an important study of the subject, had a good deal more to do with the *composition* of upcoming broadcasts than it did with the fragments of news making their way back to the studios. Reporters had to consider how they ought to introduce those stark new pieces of information. They had "breaking news," to be sure, but at the same time that news was breaking the narrative flow of already designed presentations. It was almost as if those fragments could not be offered as "news" until programmers had found a broader framework in which to place them. See Bernie Cook, *Flood of Images: Media, Memory, and Hurricane Katrina* (Austin: University of Texas Press, 2015).

3. NASA, Jet Propulsion Laboratory, California Institute of Technology, "New Study Maps Rate of New Orleans Sinking," May 16, 2016, https://www.jpl.nasa .gov/news/news.php?feature=6513 (accessed July 25, 2017).

4. Kathleen Tierney, *The Social Roots of Risk: Producing Disasters, Promoting Resilience* (Redwood City, CA: Stanford Business Books, 2014).

5. Ivor van Heerden and Mike Bryan, *The Storm: What Went Wrong and Why during Hurricane Katrina: The Inside Story from One Louisiana Scientist* (New York: Penguin Group, 2006), p. 82.

6. Dan Baum, "The Lost Year: Behind the Failure to Rebuild," *The New Yorker*, August 13, 2006, https://www.newyorker.com/magazine/2006/08/21/the-lost -year (accessed July 25, 2019).

7. For further challenges to the notion of Katrina as a "natural" disaster, see Robert D. Bullard and Beverly Wright, eds., *Race, Place, and Environmental Justice after Hurricane Katrina* (Boulder, CO: Westview Press, 2009); Chester Hartman and Gregory D. Squires, eds., *There Is No Such Thing as a Natural Disaster: Race, Class, and Hurricane Katrina* (New York: Routledge, 2006).

8. Stacy Seicshnaydre, Robert A. Collins, Cashauna Hill, and Maxwell Ciardullo, "The New Orleans Prosperity Index: Tricentennial Collection: Rigging the Real Estate Market: Segregation, Inequality, and Disaster Risk," The Data Center, April 2018, https://s3.amazonaws.com/gnocdc/reports/TDC-prosperity-brief -stacy-seicshnaydre-et-al-FINAL.pdf (accessed July 26, 2019).

9. Rivlin, *Katrina: After the Flood*, p. 78.

10. Alice Fothergill and Lori Peek, *Children of Katrina* (Austin: University of Texas Press, 2015), p. 7.

11. Michael Eric Dyson, *Come Hell or High Water: Hurricane Katrina and the Color of Disaster* (New York: Basic Civitas, 2006), p. 5.

12. Ibid.

13. Rivlin, *Katrina: After the Flood*.

14. John M. Broder, "Amid Criticism of Federal Efforts, Charges of Racism are Lodged," *New York Times*, September 5, 2005, https://www.nytimes.com/2005 /09/05/us/nationalspecial/amid-criticism-of-federal-efforts-charges-of -racism-are.html (accessed December 11, 2021).

15. "Some Can't Evacuate New Orleans for Ivan," Associated Press, September 15, 2004, https://www.wfmynews2.com/article/weather/some-cant-evacuate -new-orleans-for-ivan/83-402286717 (accessed January 4, 2020).

16. In pre-Katrina New Orleans, 5 percent of non-Latino Whites and 27 percent of Black people had no car. Dyson, *Come Hell or High Water*, p. 6.

17. Elizabeth Fussell, "Help from Family, Friends, and Strangers during Hurricane Katrina: Finding the Limits of Social Networks," in Weber and Peek, eds., *Displaced: Life in the Katrina Diaspora*, pp. 150–166.

18. Lynn Weber and Lori Peek, "Documenting Displacement: An Introduction," in Weber and Peek, eds., *Displaced: Life in the Katrina Diaspora*, pp. 1–20, p. 1.

19. Quoted in Sadie F. Dingfelder, "How Important Is Choice?," *Monitor on Psychology* 41, no. 4 (2010): 40.

20. US House of Representatives, *A Failure of Initiative: Final Report of the Select Bipartisan Committee to Investigate the Preparation for and Response to Hurricane Katrina*, vol. 109 (Washington, DC: US Government Printing, 2006), https://www.nrc.gov/docs/ML1209/ML12093A081.pdf (accessed July 25, 2019).

21. Terry W. Cole and Kelli L. Fellows, "Risk Communication Failure: A Case Study of New Orleans and Hurricane Katrina," *Southern Communication Journal* 73, no. 3 (2008): 211–228.

22. "Scores of patient deaths" were reported after Katrina, and at one point the state of Louisiana was investigating six hospitals and thirteen nursing homes for possible negligence. At least twenty-two elderly people died in eastern New Orleans at the Lafon Nursing Home, a facility run by Catholic nuns.

Another thirty-five residents died, some by drowning while still in their beds, in St. Rita's Nursing Home in St. Bernard Parish. At the end of the tumultuous trial that ensued, the owners of St. Rita's were acquitted of negligent homicide and cruelty charges. After the verdict was issued, the daughter of one of the victims at St. Rita's said, "The jury may not have found them guilty, but our savior says they are. When they face our maker, they'll have to answer then." She continued, "They still never said they were sorry. They haven't said, 'I'm sorry I let your mother drown like a rat.' They're guilty as hell." Associated Press, "Katrina Nursing Home Owners Acquitted," *NBC News*, September 7, 2007, https://www.nbcnews.com/id/wbna20649744 (accessed November 29, 2021).

23. In her Pulitzer Prize–winning book, Sheri Fink writes of doctors and nurses who stayed behind and were stuck in flooded healthcare facilities with no running water, no working sewer systems, no power, and dwindling supplies; they were forced to ration medicine and designate some patients as "last to be rescued." After days of trying to provide care in increasingly dire conditions, medical personnel began issuing lethal doses of morphine to critically ill patients in the belief that they would not survive a boat or air rescue attempt. Sheri Fink, *Five Days at Memorial: Life and Death in a Storm-Ravaged Hospital* (New York: Crown Publishing Group, 2016).

24. Nancy Gibbs, "An American Tragedy: The Aftermath," *Time*, September 12, 2005, p. 1.

25. Ibid., p. 10.

26. Jesse Walker, "Nightmare in New Orleans," *Reason*, September 7, 2005, https://reason.com/2005/09/07/nightmare-in-new-orleans-2 (accessed July 25, 2019).

27. Bruce Nolan, "Evacuations Mandatory in New Orleans," *New Orleans Times-Picayune*, September 8, 2005.

28. Tricia Wachtendorf and James M. Kendra, "Improvising Disaster in the City of Jazz: Organizational Response to Hurricane Katrina," Social Science Research Council, June 11, 2006, https://items.ssrc.org/understanding-katrina/improvising-disaster-in-the-city-of-jazz-organizational-response-to-hurricane-katrina (accessed November 29, 2021).

29. Chris Arnold, "Coast Guard Praised for Katrina Response," National Public Radio, September 9, 2005, https://www.npr.org/templates/story/story.php?storyId=4838677 (accessed July 24, 2019).

30. Greg Smith, "The Aftermath of Hurricane Katrina—A Message from Greg Smith, Director of the USGS National Wetlands Research Center in Lafayette, Louisiana," US Geological Survey, September 9, 2005, https://www.usgs.gov/about/organization/science-support/human-capital/aftermath-hurricane-katrina (accessed July 25, 2019).

31. Bob Marshall, "Game Wardens to the Rescue," *New Orleans Times-Picayune*, September 7, 2005.

32. Bob Marshall, "The Rescue Wardens," *Field & Stream* (November 2005): 21.

33. Jan Moller, "Special Needs Residents to Be Transferred to Baton Rouge," *New Orleans Times-Picayune*, August 30, 2005.

34. In some of the greatest acts of ingenuity that followed the storm, young people assembled makeshift flotation devices out of large pieces of Styrofoam or any other buoyant contraption they could find, ultimately helping to protect some of the frailest among them. For instance, one twelve-year-old boy placed his four-year-old brother, his grandmother, and his wheelchair-bound uncle on a mattress and floated them to a house with a second story when the flood-waters from Katrina got too high. Another adolescent boy used a bedsheet to tie his baby sister to his mother's waist. As they descended the steps of their flooded apartment, the boy helped his mother, who was completely distraught and did not know how to swim, navigate the contaminated waters. It was his resourcefulness that ensured their survival as he brought his family to higher ground. For more examples, see Fothergill and Peek, *Children of Katrina*; Jennifer Kirschke and Willem van Vliet, "'How Can They Look So Happy?' Reconstructing the Place of Children after Hurricane Katrina: Images and Re-flections," *Children, Youth, and Environments* 14, no. 2 (2005): 378–391.

35. "How Citizens Turned into Saviors after Katrina Struck," CBS News, August 29, 2015, https://www.cbsnews.com/news/remembering-the-cajun-navy-10-years-after-hurricane-katrina (accessed July 25, 2019).

36. Post-disaster prosocial behavior and authorities' responses to it have long been of interest to disaster researchers. For further discussion of the volunteers who rushed to New Orleans after Katrina, see Havidán Rodríguez, Joseph Trainor, and Enrico Quarantelli, "Rising to the Challenges of Catastrophe: The Emergent and Prosocial Behavior Following Hurricane Katrina," *Annals of the American Academy of Political and Social Science* 604, no. 1 (2006): 82–101.

37. Henry W. Fischer III, *Response to Disaster: Fact versus Fiction and Its Perpetuation*, 3rd ed. (Lanham, MD: University Press of America, 2008).

38. Joseph B. Treaster, "Life-or-Death Words of the Day in a Battered City: 'I Had to Get Out,'" *New York Times*, August 31, 2005, https://www.nytimes.com/2005/08/31/us/nationalspecial/lifeordeath-words-of-the-day-in-a-battered-city-i-had-to.html (accessed July 25, 2019).

39. Robert D. McFadden and Ralph Blumenthal, "Higher Death Toll Seen; Police Ordered to Stop Looters," *New York Times*, September 1, 2005, https://www.nytimes.com/2005/09/01/us/nationalspecial/higher-death-toll-seen-police-ordered-to-stop-looters.html (accessed July 24, 2019).

40. Guy Gugliotta and Peter Whoriskey, "Floods Ravage New Orleans," *Washington Post*, August 31, 2005, https://www.washingtonpost.com/archive/politics/2005/08/31/floods-ravage-new-orleans/94ee4643-4a36-4d5b-aa14-b4a52cc2 6b9c/?noredirect=on&utm_term=.feb6cf1b13a1 (accessed July 25, 2019).

41. Kevin McGill, "Officials Throw up Hands as Looters Ransack City," *Black Hills Pioneer*, August 31, 2005, https://www.bhpioneer.com/officials-throw-up-hands-as-looters-ransack-city/article_4c9089e3-51ab-5863-8d58-b2f546bbfe2f.html (accessed July 1, 2019).

42. "Troops Told 'Shoot to Kill' in New Orleans," ABC News, September 2,

2005, https://www.abc.net.au/news/2005-09-02/troops-told-shoot-to-kill-in
-new-orleans/2094678 (accessed July 25, 2019).

43. Kathleen Tierney, Christine Bevc, and Erica Kuligowski, "Metaphors Matter:
Disaster Myths, Media Frames, and Their Consequences in Hurricane
Katrina," *Annals of the American Academy of Political and Social Science* 604,
no. 1 (2006): 57–81.

44. Dexter Thomas, "When Kanye West Told George Bush That Black Lives Matter,"
Los Angeles Times, August 28, 2015, https://www.latimes.com/entertainment
/music/posts/la-et-ms-kanye-west-katrina-anniversary-george-bush-black
-lives-matter-20150827-htmlstory.html (accessed December 30, 2020).

45. Harold Toussaint, interview, Saddest Days Oral History Collection, 2005–2007;
see also D'Ann R. Penner, *Overcoming Katrina: African American Voices from
the Crescent City and Beyond* (London: Palgrave Macmillan, 2009).

46. Rivlin, *Katrina: After the Flood*, p. 130.

47. See also Steve Kroll-Smith, *Recovering Inequality: Hurricane Katrina, the San
Francisco Earthquake of 1906, and the Aftermath of Disaster* (Austin: University of Texas Press, 2018).

48. Maureen Dowd, "United States of Shame," *New York Times*, September 3, 2005,
https://www.nytimes.com/2005/09/03/opinion/united-states-of-shame.html
(accessed July 25, 2019).

49. Cited in Timothy Brezina and Joanne M. Kaufman, "What Really Happened
in New Orleans? Estimating the Threats of Violence during the Hurricane Katrina Disaster," *Justice Quarterly* 25, no. 4 (2008): 701–722.

50. Cited in David Carr, "More Horrible Than Truth: News Reports," *New York
Times*, September 19, 2005, https://www.nytimes.com/2005/09/19/business
/media/more-horrible-than-truth-news-reports.html (accessed July 25, 2019).

51. Cited in Lisa Grow Sun, "Disaster Mythology and Availability Cascades," *Duke
Environmental Law and Policy Forum* 23, no. 1 (2012): 73–92.

52. Dan Baum, "Deluged," *The New Yorker*, January 1, 2006, https://www.newyorker
.com/magazine/2006/01/09/deluged (accessed July 25, 2019).

53. "Troops Told 'Shoot to Kill' in New Orleans," ABC News, September 2, 2005,
https://www.abc.net.au/news/2005-09-02/troops-told-shoot-to-kill-in-new
-orleans/2094678 (accessed July 25, 2019).

54. Nancy Gibbs, "The Nightmare after Katrina," *Time*, September 12, 2005.

55. Ellen Barry Scott and Stephen Braun, "New Orleans Slides into Chaos: US
Scrambles to Send Troops," *Los Angeles Times*, September 2, 2005.

56. Paula Zahn, "Desperation in New Orleans; Interview with FEMA," CNN
News, September 1, 2005, http://edition.cnn.com/TRANSCRIPTS/0509/01
/pzn.01.html (accessed July 25, 2019).

57. Quoted in W. Joseph Campbell, *Getting It Wrong: Debunking the Greatest
Myths in American Journalism*, 2nd ed. (Berkeley: University of California
Press, 2016), p. 205.

58. Ibid.

59. Ibid.
60. Carr, "More Horrible Than Truth."
61. Brian Thevenot, "Myth-Making in New Orleans," *American Journalism Review* (December/January 2006), https://ir.stonybrook.edu/xmlui/handle/11401/9800 (accessed September 23, 2020).
62. Ibid.
63. For a full transcript, see "Katrina Media Coverage," *PBS NewsHour*, September 29, https://www.pbs.org/newshour/show/katrina-media-coverage (accessed December 24, 2019).
64. Jim Dwyer and Christopher Drew, "Fear Exceeded Crime's Reality in New Orleans," *New York Times*, September 29, 2005, https://www.nytimes.com /2005/09/29/us/nationalspecial/fear-exceeded-crimes-reality-in-new -orleans.html (accessed July 20, 2019).
65. Kathleen Tierney and Christine Bevc, "Disaster as War: Militarism and the Social Construction of Disaster in New Orleans," in *The Sociology of Katrina: Perspectives on a Modern Catastrophe*, edited by David L. Brunsma, David Overfelt, and J. Steven Picou, pp. 35–49 (Lanham, MD: Rowman and Little-field, 2007), p. 43.
66. Marvin Olasky, *The Politics of Disaster: Katrina, Big Government, and a New Strategy for Future Crises* (Nashville, TN: W Publishing Group, 2006), p. 25.
67. Campbell, *Getting It Wrong*, p. 202.
68. Heather Digby Parton, " 'New Orleans Was Primed for All-Out Combat': Re-membering the Media's Deadly Hurricane Katrina Racism," *Salon*, August 31, 2005, https://www.salon.com/2015/08/31/new_orleans_was_primed_for_all _out_combat_remembering_the_medias_deadly_hurricane_katrina_racism (accessed July 26, 2019).
69. Harold Toussaint, interview, Saddest Days Oral History Collection, 2005–2007; see also Penner, *Overcoming Katrina*.
70. Baum, "Deluged."
71. Susannah Rosenblatt and James Rainey. "Katrina Takes a Toll on Truth, News Accuracy," *Los Angeles Times*, September 27, 2005, https://www.latimes.com /archives/la-xpm-2005-sep-27-na-rumors27-story.html (accessed July 25, 2019).
72. Ann Scott Tyson, "Troops Back from Iraq Find Another War Zone in New Or-leans, 'It's Like Baghdad on a Bad Day,' " *Washington Post*, September 6, 2005.
73. Tierney and Bevc, "Disaster as War," p. 41.
74. The sociologists Lee Clarke and Caron Chess observe that attributions of panic in disaster are almost exclusively directed at members of the general public, but elites, they convincingly argue, often cause panic and panic them-selves during times of crisis. See Lee Clarke and Caron Chess. "Elites and Panic: More to Fear than Fear Itself," *Social Forces* 87, no. 2 (2008): 993–1014.
75. Brian Thevenot and Gordon Russell. "Rumors of Deaths Greatly Exaggerated," *New Orleans Times-Picayune*, September 26, 2005.
76. Rivlin, *Katrina: After the Flood*, p. 44.

77. Quoted in Michelle Miles and Duke W. Austin, "The Color(s) of Crisis: How Race, Rumor, and Collective Memory Shape the Legacy of Katrina," in *Racing the Storm: Racial Implications and Lessons Learned from Hurricane Katrina*, edited by Hillary Potter, pp. 33–50 (Lanham, MD: Lexington Books, 2007), p. 40.

78. Quoted in Douglas Brinkley, *The Great Deluge: Hurricane Katrina, New Orleans, and the Mississippi Gulf Coast* (New York: HarperCollins, 2006), p. 481.

79. Dwyer and Drew, "Fear Exceeded Crime's Reality in New Orleans."

80. Jessica Warner Pardee, *Surviving Katrina: The Experiences of Low-Income African American Women* (Boulder, CO: Lynne Rienner Publishers, 2014), p. 101.

81. Ibid., p. 105.

82. Ibid., p. 107.

83. Joseph B. Treaster, "Superdome: Haven Quickly Becomes an Ordeal," *New York Times*, September 1, 2005, https://www.nytimes.com/2005/09/01/us/national special/superdome-haven-quicklybecomes-an-ordeal.html (accessed July 25, 2019).

84. Although the survivors of Katrina were subject to vile misrepresentation and countless indignities, most credible accounts agree that they offered care and support to one another. In the New Orleans Convention Center, for example, the chairs left behind were arranged in hundreds of small circles—people had, on their own, formed up into small groups of families and friends, protecting each other. See William P. Quigley, "What Katrina Revealed," *Harvard Law and Policy Review* 2, no. 2 (2008): 361–384, p. 377.

85. John Burnett, "Evacuees Were Turned Away at Gretna, La.," National Public Radio, September 20, 2005, https://www.npr.org/templates/story/story.php ?storyId=4855611 (accessed November 29, 2021).

86. Baum, "Deluged."

87. Ibid.

88. Quoted from Stephen J. Lyons, *The 1,000 Year Flood: Destruction, Loss, Rescue, and Redemption along the Mississippi River* (Guilford, CT: Globe Pequot, 2010).

89. This point has been well made by scholars who have come before us. Social scientists, in particular, were quick and withering in their critiques of the racially charged media coverage of Katrina. For just one example among many, see Dyson, *Come Hell or High Water*.

90. Ron Eyerman, *Is This America? Katrina as Cultural Trauma* (Austin: University of Texas Press, 2015).

91. Rivlin, *Katrina: After the Flood*, p. 359.

92. Nicholas Lehmann, "The New New Orleans," *New York Review of Books*, March 24, 2011.

93. Alex de Waal, "An Imperfect Storm: Narratives of Calamity in a Liberal-Technocratic Age," Social Science Research Council, June 11, 2006, https:// items.ssrc.org/understanding-katrina/an-imperfect-storm-narratives-of -calamity-in-a-liberal-technocratic-age (accessed November 29, 2021).

94. Campbell, *Getting It Wrong*, pp. 4, 10. Thevenot went on, however, to attribute the widespread journalistic errors and omissions to a "devastated communications apparatus." Because he framed the reporting failures as having emerged from the chaos of the disaster itself, the lessons he offered for journalists remained at that level as well. Rigorously fact-check your sources. Offer qualifications when you have not yet been able to fully verify an account. Write corrections when they are warranted, and make the corrections themselves the main story. The issue with this approach lies in the lack of acknowledgment of the *root causes* of the widespread media failures. Thevenot identified poor, Black flood victims and local Black leaders as the primary sources of the myths that the press so vigorously reported. While he recognized that these groups were in no way immune from the broader cultural climate that regularly dehumanizes African Americans as threatening outsiders, Thevenot simply concluded, without a hint of irony: "I don't think race was an overriding factor." In the end, he rejected the explanatory power of race and social class, two defining characteristics that sociologists have long argued shape nearly all aspects of social life, including media representations.

95. Quoted in Susannah Rosenblatt and James Rainey, "Katrina Takes a Toll on Truth, News Accuracy," *Los Angeles Times*, September 27, 2005, https://www.latimes.com/archives/la-xpm-2005-sep-27-na-rumors27-story.html (accessed July 25, 2019).

96. A. C. Thompson, "Post-Katrina, White Vigilantes Shot African Americans with Impunity," *ProPublica*, December 19, 2008, https://www.propublica.org/article/post-katrina-white-vigilantes-shot-african-americans-with-impunity (accessed July 25, 2019).

97. Ibid.

98. Ibid.

99. Ibid.

PART II: LOCATING KATRINA

1. Eric S. Blake, Christopher W. Landsea, and Ethan J. Gibney, "The Deadliest, Costliest, and Most Intense United States Tropical Cyclones from 1851 to 2010 (and Other Frequently Requested Hurricane Facts)." NOAA Technical Memorandum NWS NHC-6 (August 2011), https://www.nhc.noaa.gov/pdf/nws-nhc-6.pdf (accessed January 1, 2020).

2. Carl Bialik, "We Still Don't Know How Many People Died Because of Katrina," *FiveThirtyEight*, August 26, 2015, https://fivethirtyeight.com/features/we-still-dont-know-how-many-people-died-because-of-katrina (accessed January 1, 2020). For more information on the missing and deceased in Katrina, see Joan Brunkard, Gonza Namulanda, and Raoult Ratard, "Hurricane Katrina Deaths, Louisiana, 2005," *Disaster Medicine and Public Health Preparedness* 2, no. 4

(2008): 215–223; and Patrick Sharkey, "Survival and Death in New Orleans: An Empirical Look at the Human Impact of Katrina," *Journal of Black Studies* 37, no. 4 (2007): 482–501.

3. Allison Plyer, "Facts for Features: Katrina Impact," Greater New Orleans Community Data Center, August 26, 2014, https://www.datacenterresearch.org/data-resources/katrina/facts-for-impact (accessed July 2, 2019).

4. Charles E. Fritz, "Disasters," in *Contemporary Social Problems*, edited by Robert K. Merton and Robert A. Nisbet, pp. 651–694 (New York: Harcourt, 1961), p. 655.

CHAPTER 3: IN TIME

1. Louisiana Coastal Wetlands Planning Protection and Restoration Act Program, "The Mississippi River Delta Basin," https://lacoast.gov/new/About/Basin_data/mr (accessed July 26, 2019).

2. Louisiana Department of Environmental Quality, *The Louisiana Regional Restoration Planning Program: Final Programmatic Environmental Impact Statement*, January 2007, http://www.losco.state.la.us/pdf_docs/FPEIS_RRPProgram.pdf (accessed July 26, 2019).

3. Ari Kelman, *A River and Its City: The Nature of Landscape in New Orleans* (Berkeley: University of California Press, 2003), p. 148.

4. "Industrial Canal and Inner Harbor," *New Orleans States Item*, July 27, 1943, special insert, p. 21.

5. Freudenburg et al., *Catastrophe in the Making*.

6. Freudenburg and Gramling, *Blowout in the Gulf*.

7. Ivor van Heerden and Mike Bryan, *The Storm: What Went Wrong and Why during Hurricane Katrina: The Inside Story from One Louisiana Scientist* (New York: Penguin Group, 2006), p. 161.

8. Freudenburg et al., *Catastrophe in the Making*, p. 119.

9. Louisiana Wildlife and Fisheries Commission, "Statement of Louisiana Wildlife and Fisheries Commission Relative to New Orleans to the Gulf Tidewater Channel," September 16 and 17, 1957.

10. Freudenburg et al., *Catastrophe in the Making*.

11. Ivor L. van Heerden, G. Paul Kemp, Wes Shrum, Ezra Boyd, and Hassan Mashriqui, "Initial Assessment of the New Orleans Flooding Event during the Passage of Hurricane Katrina" (Baton Rouge: Louisiana State University, Center for the Study of Public Health Impacts of Hurricanes, 2005), p. 4.

12. US Geological Survey, "Louisiana's Rate of Coastal Wetland Loss Continues to Slow," July 12, 2017, https://www.usgs.gov/news/usgs-louisiana-s-rate-coastal-wetland-loss-continues-slow (accessed March 12, 2019).

13. Freudenburg et al., *Catastrophe in the Making*, p. 117.

14. Lionel D. Lyles and Fulbert Namwamba, "Louisiana Coastal Zone Erosion: 100+ Years of Landuse and Land Loss Using GIS and Remote Sensing," in

Proceedings of the Fifth Annual ESRI Education User Conference (San Diego, 2005), pp. 23–26, http://proceedings.esri.com/library/userconf/educo5/papers/pap1222.pdf (accessed July 26, 2019).

15. Ibid.

16. Quoted in Kevin McGill, "La. Flood Board Sues Oil Companies over Erosion," Associated Press, July 24, 2013, https://www.apnews.com/efff5c98b5124084a7f6d0f1786633e3 (accessed July 26, 2019).

17. 100 Resilient Cities, "New Orleans Preliminary Resilience Assessment," June 2015, https://www.nola.gov/resilience/resources/nola-preliminary-resilience-assessment-6-15 (accessed July 26, 2019).

18. Freudenburg et al., *Catastrophe in the Making*, p. 130.

19. Ibid, p. 141.

20. William R. Freudenburg, Robert Gramling, Shirley Laska, and Kai T. Erikson, "Disproportionality and Disaster: Hurricane Katrina and the Mississippi River-Gulf Outlet," *Social Science Quarterly* 90, no. 3 (2009): 497–515.

21. US Army Corps of Engineers (USACE), *Performance Evaluation of the New Orleans and Southeast Louisiana Hurricane Protection System: Final Report of the Interagency Performance Evaluation Task Force*, June 2009, https://biotech.law.lsu.edu/katrina/ipet/Volume%20I%20FINAL%2023Jun09%20mh.pdf (accessed July 26, 2019). It is worth noting that the Lake Borgne surge barrier, completed in 2013, is an attempt to reduce the marsh-killing salinity introduced by the MRGO.

22. For a historical account of Katrina, see Andy Horowitz, *Katrina: A History, 1915–2015* (Cambridge, MA: Harvard University Press, 2020).

23. Knabb, Rhome, and Brown, "Tropical Cyclone Report: Hurricane Katrina, 23–30 August 2005."

24. Mary Alice Mills, Donald Edmondson, and Crystal L. Park, "Trauma and Stress Response among Hurricane Katrina Evacuees," *American Journal of Public Health* 97, no. 1 (2007): S116-S123.

25. Katherine Browne, *Standing in the Need: Culture, Comfort, and Coming Home after Katrina* (Austin: University of Texas Press, 2015).

26. The Road Home program offered grants to homeowners like Katie, but no support to renters—who made up half the pre-Katrina population and were disproportionately Black. Even with the support of the program, Black homeowners received less compensation than their White counterparts owing to program rules, arbitrary grant formulas, cloudy titles, and lower property values, all of which are the legacy of redlining and other racist housing policies. For more on the failures of the Road Home program, see Horowitz, *Katrina: A History*.

27. Ernest E. Sullivent III, Christine A. West, Rebecca S. Noe, Karen E. Thomas, L. J. David Wallace, and Rebecca T. Leeb, "Nonfatal Injuries Following Hurricane Katrina—New Orleans, Louisiana, 2005," *Journal of Safety Research* 37, no. 2 (2006): 213–217.

28. Hurricane Katrina Community Advisory Group and Ronald C. Kessler, "Hurricane Katrina's Impact on the Care of Survivors with Chronic Medical Conditions," *Journal of General Internal Medicine* 22, no. 9 (2007): 1225–1230.

29. Ronald C. Kessler, Sandro Galea, Russell T. Jones, and Holly A. Parker, "Mental Illness and Suicidality after Hurricane Katrina," *Bulletin of the World Health Organization* 84, no. 12 (2006): 930–939.

30. J. Steven Picou and Keith Nicholls, *Caught in the Path of Katrina: A Survey of the Hurricane's Human Effects* (Austin: University of Texas Press, 2019).

31. Katy Reckdahl, "The Dark Side of Katrina Recovery," *Politico*, August 31, 2015, https://www.politico.com/magazine/story/2015/08/katrina-inequality-race-new-orleans-213087 (accessed March 17, 2019).

CHAPTER 4: IN SPACE

1. For further discussion, see Kai Erikson, *The Sociologist's Eye: Reflections on Social Life* (New Haven, CT: Yale University Press, 2018).

2. Weber and Peek, "Documenting Displacement."

3. Rivlin, *Katrina: After the Flood.*

4. Taunya Lovell Banks, "Post-Katrina Suppression of Black Working-Class Political Expression," *Journal of Public Management and Social Policy* 22, no. 2 (2015): 1–11.

5. Rivlin, *Katrina: After the Flood*, p. 56.

6. Ibid., p. 180.

7. From the meeting notes of the SSRC Task Force on Hurricane Katrina, New York, November 12, 2010.

8. Quoted in Andrew Horowitz, "The End of Empire, Louisiana: Disaster and Recovery on the Gulf Coast, 1915–2012," PhD diss., Yale University, Department of History, 2014.

9. David Brooks, "Katrina's Silver Lining," *New York Times*, September 8, 2005, https://www.nytimes.com/2005/09/08/opinion/katrinas-silver-lining.html (accessed February 26, 2019).

10. Much of Gladwell's argument depended on social science data focused on the prospects of those who were released from prison just prior to Katrina. He had few words to say about the elderly, single mothers, or persons with disabilities who were the least likely to return to New Orleans. As such, Gladwell conflated the life chances of those people who had been convicted of a crime and recently paroled with those of the ordinary residents of New Orleans, never pausing to consider that the social networks of the two groups might be radically different. Therefore, to disrupt one would not necessarily have the same meaning as to sever the other. See Malcolm Gladwell, "Starting Over: Many Katrina Victims Left New Orleans for Good. What Can We Learn from Them?" *The New Yorker*, August 17, 2015, https://www.newyorker.com/magazine/2015/08/24/starting-over-dept-of-social-studies-malcolm-gladwell (accessed January 2, 2020).

11. Kristen Buras, "Race, Charter Schools, and Conscious Capitalism: On the Spatial Politics of Whiteness as Property (and the Unconscionable Assault on Black New Orleans)," *Harvard Educational Review* 81, no. 2 (2011): 296–331.

12. William P. Quigley, "Katrina Voting Wrongs: Aftermath of Hurricane and Weak Enforcement Dilute African American Voting Rights in New Orleans," *Washington and Lee Journal of Civil Rights and Social Justice* 14, no. 1 (2007): 49–75.

13. Jonathan Tilove, "Louisiana's 40-Year Streak in Backing Presidential Winner Comes to an End," *New Orleans Times-Picayune*, November 5, 2008, https://www.nola.com/news/article_fadfe188-f18c-5068-90d8-2246301c2fea.html (accessed July 26, 2019).

14. Jessica Warner Pardee, *Surviving Katrina: The Experiences of Low-Income African American Women* (Boulder, CO: Lynne Rienner Press, 2014).

15. Quigley, "What Katrina Revealed."

16. Cindi Katz, "Bad Elements: Katrina and the Scoured Landscape of Social Reproduction," *Gender, Place, and Culture* 15, no. 1 (2008): 15–29.

17. Susan Saulny, "5,000 Public Housing Units in New Orleans Are to Be Razed," *New York Times*, June 15, 2006, https://www.nytimes.com/2006/06/15/us/15housing.html (accessed June 19, 2019).

18. John Harwood, "Louisiana Lawmakers Aim to Cope with Political Fallout," *Wall Street Journal*, September 9, 2006, https://www.wsj.com/articles/SB112622923108136137 (accessed May 26, 2019).

19. Jane Arnold Lincove, Nathan Barrett, and Katharine O. Strunk, "Lessons from Hurricane Katrina: The Employment Effects of the Mass Dismissal of New Orleans Teachers," *Educational Researcher* 47, no. 3 (2018): 191–203.

20. Kenneth Brad Ott, "The Closure of New Orleans' Charity Hospital after Hurricane Katrina: A Case of Disaster Capitalism," master's thesis, University of New Orleans, Department of Sociology, May 18, 2012, https://scholarworks.uno.edu/td/1472.

21. Kristina Kay Robinson, "What's Old Is New Again," *Guernica*, April 22, 2015, https://www.guernicamag.com/kristina-kay-robinson-whats-old-is-new-again (accessed December 1, 2021).

22. William W. Falk, Matthew O. Hunt, and Larry L. Hunt, "Hurricane Katrina and New Orleanians' Sense of Place: Return and Reconstitution or 'Gone with the Wind'?" *Du Bois Review: Social Science Research on Race* 3, no. 1 (2006): 115–128.

23. Kalamu ya Salaam, interview with Joshua Guild, June 5, 2006, interview U-0264, Southern Oral History Program Collection no. 4007, https://docsouth.unc.edu/sohp/html_use/U-0264.html (accessed July 26, 2019).

24. For more on the effects of the post-disaster displacement, see Vincanne Adams, Taslim Van Hattum, and Diana English, "Chronic Disaster Syndrome: Displacement, Disaster Capitalism, and the Eviction of the Poor from New Orleans," *American Ethnologist* 36, no. 4 (2009): 615–636.

25. Rivlin, *Katrina: After the Flood*, p. 398.

26. Mindy Thompson Fullilove, *Root Shock: How Tearing Up City Neighborhoods Hurts America, and What We Can Do about It* (Oakland, CA: New Village Press, 2016).

27. Baum, "The Lost Year."

28. Elizabeth Fussell, "Leaving New Orleans: Social Stratification, Networks, and Hurricane Evacuation," Social Science Research Council, June 11, 2006, https://items.ssrc.org/understanding-katrina/leaving-new-orleans-social -stratification-networks-and-hurricane-evacuation/ (accessed November 29, 2021).

CHAPTER 5: BEFORE

1. William James, *Memories and Studies* (New York: Longmans and Green, 1911), p. 212.
2. Kai T. Erikson, *Everything in Its Path: Destruction of Community in the Buffalo Creek Flood* (1976) (New York: Simon & Schuster, 2006), p. v.
3. Ibid.
4. Alice Fothergill and Lori Peek, "Poverty and Disasters in the United States: A Review of Recent Sociological Findings," *Natural Hazards* 32, no. 1 (2004): 89–110.
5. Researchers have drawn such maps that show where the socially vulnerable are most likely to reside. For two prominent examples, see Agency for Toxic Substances and Disease Registry (ATSDR), "CDC/ATSDR Social Vulnerability Index," https://www.atsdr.cdc.gov/placeandhealth/svi/index.html; and University of South Carolina, Hazards and Vulnerability Institute, "Social Vulnerability Index for the United States—2010–2014," http://artsandsciences .sc.edu/geog/hvri/sovi%C2%AE-0.
6. Fothergill and Peek, "Poverty and Disasters in the United States."
7. Junia Howell and James Elliott, "As Disaster Costs Rise, So Does Inequality," *Socius: Sociological Research for a Dynamic World*, December 4, 2018, https:// doi.org/10.1177/2378023118816795.
8. Laura Lein, Ronald Angel, Julie Beausoleil, and Holly Bell, "The Basement of Extreme Poverty: Katrina Survivors and Poverty Programs," in Weber and Peek, eds., *Displaced: Life in the Katrina Diaspora*, pp. 47–62.
9. Javier Auyero and Débora Alejandra Swistun, *Flammable: Environmental Suffering in an Argentine Shantytown* (Oxford: Oxford University Press, 2009).
10. Fothergill and Peek collected several narratives from children after Hurricane Katrina, where they repeated their belief that "levees had been blown" to save the White sections of the city, while sacrificing the areas home to Black residents. Fothergill and Peek, *Children of Katrina*.
11. During the 1927 Mississippi River flood, White business elites in New Orleans convinced Louisiana's governor to dynamite a section of the river levee. That move saved the urban core, but devastated people living in St. Bernard and Plaquemines Parishes. Those areas were home to a mix of people of African, Native American, Spanish, and French descent. See Horowitz, *Katrina: A History*.
12. Our colleague, the sociologist Jacquelyn Litt, was talking to an evacuee from New Orleans named Wendy about her family network, and Wendy referred to a close friend who was not kin in any literal sense of the word. "When we

was in New Orleans, oh yeah, I always help out with her kids and stuff. We always did help each other.... They family." That can sound like a fairly tangled web, but what it really means is that the type of feelings and obligations one has toward blood relatives can extend beyond one's genetic family to include neighbors or others who feel like, act like, and assume the responsibilities of a family. See Jacquelyn Litt, "'We Need to Get Together with Each Other': Women's Narratives of Help in Katrina's Displacement," in Weber and Peek, eds., *Displaced: Life in the Katrina Diaspora*, pp. 167–182, 170.

13. For a definitive account of the Great Migration, see Isabel Wilkerson, *The Warmth of Other Suns: The Epic Story of America's Great Migration* (New York: Vintage, 2011).

14. As Moynihan became an ever more prominent spokesman on the status of family life, other scholars were offering divergent views through their written work and testimony in Congress about kin organization in Black families. These prominent scholars, who included Linda Burton, Robert Hill, Joyce Ladner, and Carol Stack, used detailed ethnographic data to show that extended families take on the work that people living in poverty need to do in order to survive. In 1993, Stack and Burton developed a kinscript framework for examining how kin, as multigenerational collectives, and the individuals embedded within them negotiate the life course.

15. Daniel Patrick Moynihan, "Chapter II: The Negro American Family," in *The Negro Family: The Case for National Action* (Washington, DC: US Department of Labor, Office of Planning and Research, 1965), https://www.dol.gov/general/aboutdol /history/webid-moynihan/moynchapter2 (accessed September 23, 2021).

16. Daniel Patrick Moynihan, "Chapter IV: The Tangle of Pathology," in *The Negro Family: The Case for National Action*, https://www.dol.gov/general/aboutdol /history/webid-moynihan/moynchapter4 (accessed September 23, 2021).

17. Ibid.

18. Those wider family circles can be far more helpful for mothers whose mates are coming of age in a world marked by systemic injustice toward Black men, who run a 50 percent chance of being unable to maintain full-time employment and are far more likely than White neighbors who behave in just the same way to be arrested and experience a term in prison. Louisiana has one of the highest rates of incarceration in the United States, and a considerable majority of those in prison at any given time are African Americans. Two blunt facts to ponder: African Americans make up 32 percent of the Louisiana population and 75 percent of the state's prison population. It is hard to imagine any crime that can make that much of a difference in incarceration rates—other than that of being born Black in a White-dominated world. See Katz, "Bad Elements."

19. Picou and Nicholls, *Caught in the Path of Katrina*.

20. Allison Helmuth and Jane M. Henrici, "Women in New Orleans: Race, Poverty, and Hurricane Katrina," Fact Sheet D490 (Washington, DC: Institute for Women's Policy Research, 2010).

21. Elizabeth Fussell, Narayan Sastry, and Mark VanLandingham, "Race, Socio-economic Status, and Return Migration to New Orleans after Hurricane Katrina," *Population and Environment* 31, nos. 1–3 (2010): 20–42.

22. Quoted in Jonas E. Alexis, *In the Name of Education: How Weird Ideologies Corrupt Our Public Schools, Politics, the Media, Higher Institutions, and History* (Maitland, FL: Xulon Press, 2007), p. 67.

23. Quoted in Clyde Woods, "Do You Know What It Means to Miss New Orleans? Katrina, Trap Economics, and the Rebirth of the Blues," *American Quarterly* 57, no. 4 (2005): 1005–1018, p. 1014.

24. Carol Stack, *All Our Kin: Strategies for Survival in a Black Community* (New York: Harper & Row, 1974).

25. Browne, *Standing in the Need*, p. 144.

26. Elaine Enarson, *Women Confronting Natural Disaster: From Vulnerability to Resilience* (Boulder, CO: Lynne Rienner, 2012).

27. Quoted in Sadie F. Dingfelder, "How Important Is Choice?" *Monitor on Psychology* 41, no. 4 (2010): 40.

28. Quoted in Nicole M. Stephens, MarYam G. Hamedani, Hazel Rose Markus, Hilary B. Bergsieker, and Liyam Eloul, "Why Did They 'Choose' to Stay? Perspectives of Hurricane Katrina Observers and Survivors," *Psychological Science* 20, no. 7 (2009): 878–886.

29. Beverly J. Mason, "The Women of Renaissance Village: From Homes in New Orleans to a Trailer Park in Baker, Louisiana," in Weber and Peek, eds., *Displaced: Life in the Katrina Diaspora*, pp. 183–197.

CHAPTER 6: DURING

1. Keith Darcé, "More Power to Them: 6,000 Utility Workers Are Here—Airport, Refineries Are First to Be Restored," *New Orleans Times-Picayune*, September 3, 2005.

2. Joseph B. Treaster, "Escaping Feared Knockout Punch, Barely, New Orleans Is One Lucky Big Mess," *New York Times*, August 30, 2005.

3. Mark Strassmann, "10 Years after Katrina, Operators Remember Agonizing 911 Calls," CBS News, August 25, 2015, https://www.cbsnews.com/news/ten-years-after-katrina-operators-remember-agonizing-911-calls (accessed December 11, 2021).

4. Quoted in Jim Garbour, "A Katrina Survivor's Tale: 'They Forgot Us and That's When Things Started to Get Bad,'" *Guardian*, August 27, 2015.

5. Jennifer Pangyanszki, "Three Days of Death, Despair, and Survival," CNN News, September 9, 2005, https://www.cnn.com/2005/US/09/09/katrina.survivors/index.html (accessed December 12, 2021).

6. Fran H. Norris and Leslie H. Wind, "The Experience of Disaster: Trauma, Loss, Adversities, and Community Effects," in *Mental Health and Disasters*, edited

by Yuval Neria, Sandro Galea, and Fran H. Norris, pp. 29–44 (Cambridge: Cambridge University Press, 2009).

7. Jimmy Smith, "Mannings Arrive, Provide Relief—Quarterbacks Receive Harrowing Tales of Misfortune, Survival," *New Orleans Times-Picayune*, September 4, 2005.

8. Joseph B. Treaster and Deborah Sontag, "Local Officials Criticize Federal Government over Response," *New York Times*, September 2, 2005.

9. Trymaine D. Lee, "Seeking Help in New Orleans, People Instead Find Death, Unrest—Rape, Gunfire Reported at Convention Center," *New Orleans Times-Picayune*, September 4, 2005.

10. Peter Applebome, Christopher Drew, Jere Longman, and Andrew C. Revkin, "A Delicate Balance Is Undone in a Flash, and a Battered City Waits," *New York Times*, September 3, 2005.

11. Ibid.

12. Robert D. McFadden, "New Orleans Begins a Search for Its Dead," *New York Times*, September 5, 2005.

13. Ibid.

14. Dyson, *Come Hell or High Water*, p. 2.

15. Applebome et al., "A Delicate Balance Is Undone in a Flash."

16. Dyson, *Come Hell or High Water*, p. 6.

17. Ibid., p. 10.

18. William Julius Wilson, *More than Just Race: Being Black and Poor in the Inner City* (New York: W. W. Norton & Co., 2009).

19. Erikson, *Everything in Its Path*.

20. Lawrence L. Langer, *Holocaust Testimonies: The Ruins of Memory* (New Haven, CT: Yale University Press, 1991), p. 59.

CHAPTER 7: AFTER

1. Executive Office of the President, *The Federal Response to Hurricane Katrina: Lessons Learned* (Washington, DC: US Government Printing Office, February 2006).

2. Mannana V. K. Sivakumar, Raymond P. Motha, and Haripada P. Das, *Natural Disaster and Extreme Events in Agriculture* (Berlin: Springer-Verlag, 2005).

3. US Census Bureau, "The Great Migration, 1910 to 1970," September 13, 2012, https://www.census.gov/dataviz/visualizations/020 (accessed September 24, 2019).

4. Wilkerson, *The Warmth of Other Suns*.

5. Narayan Sastry and Jesse Gregory, "The Location of Displaced New Orleans Residents in the Year after Hurricane Katrina," *Demography* 51, no. 3 (2014): 753–775.

6. Executive Office of the President, *The Federal Response to Hurricane Katrina: Lessons Learned*.

7. Lori Peek, Bridget Morrissey, and Holly Marlatt, "Disaster Hits Home: A Model of Displaced Family Adjustment after Hurricane Katrina," *Journal of Family Issues* 32 (2011): 1371–1396.

8. Ibid.

9. See Fothergill and Peek, *Children of Katrina*.

10. From the meeting notes of the SSRC Task Force on Hurricane Katrina, New York, November 12, 2010.

11. Peek, Morrissey, and Marlatt, "Disaster Hits Home," pp. 1386–1387.

12. Jennifer Tobin-Gurley, Lori Peek, and Jennifer Loomis, "Displaced Single Mothers in the Aftermath of Hurricane Katrina: Resource Needs and Resource Acquisition," *International Journal of Mass Emergencies and Disasters* 28, no. 2 (2010): 170–206, p. 195.

13. Weber and Peek, "Documenting Displacement," p. 14.

14. Peek, "They Call It 'Katrina Fatigue,'" p. 34.

15. For examples of how this post-disaster dynamic played out in Texas, Colorado, and South Carolina, respectively, see Lee M. Miller, "Katrina Evacuee Reception in Rural East Texas: Rethinking Disaster 'Recovery,'" in Weber and Peek, eds., *Displaced: Life in the Katrina Diaspora*, pp. 104–118; Peek, "They Call It 'Katrina Fatigue'"; and Lynn Weber, "When Demand Exceeds Supply: Disaster Response and the Southern Political Economy," in Weber and Peek, eds., *Displaced: Life in the Katrina Diaspora*, pp. 80–103.

16. Gary Rivlin, "White New Orleans Has Recovered from Hurricane Katrina. Black New Orleans Has Not," *Talk Poverty*, August 29, 2016, https://talkpoverty.org/2016/08/29/white-new-orleans-recovered-hurricane-katrina-black-new-orleans-not/ (accessed September 23, 2021).

17. Tobin-Gurley, Peek, and Loomis, "Displaced Single Mothers in the Aftermath of Hurricane Katrina."

18. From the meeting notes of the SSRC Task Force on Hurricane Katrina, New York, November 12, 2010.

19. Browne, *Standing in the Need*.

20. Litt, "'We Need to Get Together with Each Other.'"

21. Fussell, "Help from Family, Friends, and Strangers during Hurricane Katrina."

22. Steve Kroll-Smith, Vern Baxter, and Pam Jenkins, *Left to Chance: Hurricane Katrina and the Story of Two New Orleans Neighborhoods* (Austin: University of Texas Press, 2015), p. 79.

23. Ibid., p. 82.

24. Ibid., p. 115.

25. Browne, *Standing in the Need*, p. 23.

26. Ibid., p. 35.

27. Ibid., p. 129.

28. Browne writes that because the family "functioned as a collective, individual grief and collective grief came bundled together, intensifying the loss and the sorrow." Ibid., p. 36.

POSTLUDE

1. Linda Villarosa, "'A Terrible Price': The Deadly Racial Disparities of Covid-19 in America," *New York Times*, April 29, 2020, https://www.nytimes.com/2020/04/29/magazine/racial-disparities-covid-19.html (accessed June 28, 2021).
2. Centers for Disease Control and Prevention, "Risk for COVID-19 Infection, Hospitalization, and Death by Race/Ethnicity," https://www.cdc.gov/coronavirus/2019-ncov/covid-data/investigations-discovery/hospitalization-death-by-race-ethnicity.html (accessed June 28, 2021; updated July 16, 2021).
3. Erikson, *Everything in Its Path*.

ACKNOWLEDGMENTS

1. For some of the common themes across the contributions to the Katrina Bookshelf, see Steve Kroll-Smith and Rachel S. Madsen, "Disaster, Time, and Dialogue: A Couple Lessons from Hurricane Katrina," *Sociological Inquiry* 84, no. 3 (2014): 360–369.
2. For a more detailed story of the emergence of the SSRC Task Force, see Kai Erikson, "Studying Katrina," *Sociological Inquiry* 84, no. 3 (2014): 344–353.
3. For information on the formation and activities of the SSRC Research Network on Persons Displaced by Hurricane Katrina, see Lori Peek, Alice Fothergill, Jessica W. Pardee, and Lynn Weber, "Studying Displacement: New Networks, Lessons Learned," *Sociological Inquiry* 84, no. 3 (2014): 354–359.

ABOUT THE AUTHORS

Kai Erikson is the William R. Kenan, Jr. Professor Emeritus of Sociology and American Studies at Yale University. He is past president of the American Sociological Association, winner of the MacIver and Sorokin Awards from the ASA, and author of *Wayward Puritans: A Study in the Sociology of Deviance, Everything in Its Path: Destruction of Community in the Buffalo Creek Flood, A New Species of Trouble: The Human Experience of Modern Disasters*, and *The Sociologist's Eye: Reflections on Social Life*. His teaching and research interests include American communities, human disasters, and ethnonational conflict. He is the chair of the Social Science Research Council Task Force on Hurricane Katrina and series editor for the Katrina Bookshelf, published by the University of Texas Press.

Lori Peek is a professor of sociology and the director of the Natural Hazards Center at the University of Colorado Boulder. She is also the leader of the National Science Foundation–supported CONVERGE facility and of the Social Science Extreme Events Research (SSEER) and Interdisciplinary Science and Engineering Extreme Events Research (ISEEER) networks. She is co-editor of *Displaced: Life in the Katrina Diaspora*, co-author of *Children of Katrina*, author of *Behind the Backlash: Muslim Americans after 9/11*, and co-editor of the *Handbook of Environmental Sociology*. Since 2005, she has served as the associate chair of the Social Science Research Council Task Force on Hurricane Katrina.

INDEX

Page numbers in italics indicate photographs.

disabled persons, 85, 120n34
disasters, 103; Covid-19 pandemic as, xi, 107, 108; definition of, xii–xiii, 47–48; in future, 108–109; geographic dimensions of, 47–48, 61–62, 68–69; human harm from, xiii; low-income residents affected by, xiv, 74–75; personification of, 73–74; study of, xi–xii, xv, 105–106; temporal dimensions of, 47–48, 49, 56–57, 60
discrimination, 75; against low-income residents, 63, 66
disorientation: of displaced persons, 68–69, 99–100; of survivors, 7–8
displaced persons, ii, xiii; African Americans discussed as, 31; Black New Orleans residents as, 62–63, 100–101; disorientation of, 68–69, 99–100; firsthand accounts from, 96–97; Katrina fatigue toward, xv, 98–99; migrations of, 76, 95–96, 97, 99; officials' decision on, xiv–xv, 96; police blocking, 44–45; refugee term compared to, 31; structural racism against, 63–64, 65, 65, 66–67, 67, 68; in US, 95–96
Dust Bowl, 95, 96
Dyson, Michael Eric, 88, 90

earthquake (1906), 73
Eighth Ward, 74
elderly persons, 84, 87, 118n22
Este, Debbie, 84–85
evacuation: of New Orleans families, 80–81, 101; of New Orleans residents, ii, 17–18; of New Orleans residents, White, 89; and 9/11 comparison, 45; from Ninth Ward, 58; officials' stance on, 80, 81
extended family, 80–81, 133n28; benefits of, 77–78, 130n14, 130n18; Covid-19 pandemic damage to, 108; mobility of, 79–80; nuclear family compared to, 76. *See also* New Orleans families
Exxon Valdez oil spill, xv, 5

family: kin-hood compared to, 76, 79; nuclear, 76, 79, 84; separation of,

97–98, 100–101; structure of, 76–78, 130n14, 130n18. *See also* extended family; New Orleans families; support systems
fatalities, 4, 18, 40; at Convention Center, 30; firsthand accounts of, 84, 85, 87; at healthcare facilities, 118n22, 119n23; from Katrina disaster, ii, 47, 56–57; from Katrina flood, 13; military troops threat of, 34; at nursing homes, 118n22; suicide as, 56–57; at Superdome, 30; uncertainty about, 33
fathers, 77
federal disaster response: failure of, 18–19, 87; media on, 18–19; and military troop deployment, 34–35
Federal Emergency Management Agency (FEMA), 80, 102–103
Fink, Sheri, 119n23
fires, 19
firsthand accounts: of Andre (survivor), 83; of Daniels, 86; disorientation of, 7–8; of displaced persons, 96–97; of Este, 84; of fatalities, 84, 85, 87; and interviews, 90; of Toussaint, 34–35; of Weber, 85
floods: in Buffalo Creek, 73–74; in Cedar Rapids, 42; of Mississippi River (1927), 75, 129n11
flooding, Katrina: Lower Ninth Ward residents experiencing, 75, 84; New Orleans family affected by, 83, 84; survivors stranded by, 83–84, 85, 88–89, 89; timeline of, 12–13
Florida, ix, 3, 95
fossil fuels, 51–52
Fox News: focus of, 12–13; misinformation spread by, 26
Fritz, Charles, 47–48
Fussell, Elizabeth, 69, 101

Galveston hurricane, 47
Gentilly neighborhood, 74, 83
gentrification, 64, 67
Georgia, 96
Getting It Wrong (Campbell), 39
Gladwell, Malcolm, 64, 127n10
Gretna suburb, 44–45

Gulf Coast: Bush on, 3; damage to, ix–x, 3–4; livelihoods in, 9

Gulf Coast residents: human experience of, 7–8; New Orleans residents compared to, 10–11; resiliency of, 9–10

Gulf of Mexico, ix

Haitian migrant workers, 69

health-care facilities, 18, 66, 87, 118n22, 119n23

Heerden, Ivor van, 52

Henrici, Jane, 98

Hewitt, Hugh, 29

Holocaust survivors, 93

home, sense of, 68–69

homes, 5–6, 6, 7–8, 74–75, 129n5. See also housing, mixed-income; public housing

Horowitz, Andrew, 64

hospitals, 66, 118n22

housing, mixed-income, 66

humanitarian aid, 31–33, 36. See also rescue efforts

Hurricane Highway, 53

Hurricane Ida, 106–107

Hurricane Katrina: damage done by, 3–7, diaspora from, 95; 911 call center response to, 82–83; size of, ix–x, 8; trajectory shift of, x, 12

hurricanes, ix, 10. See also Galveston hurricane

Industrial Canal, 15, 51

inequality, xiv, 87–88, 105; economic, 90–91; housing vulnerability from, 74–75, 129n5. See also racial inequality

Interstate 10, 86

Jackson, Jesse, 16, 31

James, William, 73

Jones, Van, 24

journalism. See media

journalists, 60; oversight of, 43; and suicide, 57; on survivors, 86, 89

Katrina Bookshelf, ii, 105, 111, 112, 113, 123n1

Katrina fatigue, xv, 98–99, 133n15

Katz, Cindi, 65

kin-hood, 76, 79

Lake Borgne surge barrier, 126n21

Lake Pontchartrain, 13, 14

levees, x, 12, 14, 15, 18, 29, 31, 49, 51, 69, 75, 84, 85, 129n10, 129n11

Limbaugh, Rush, 42

London Financial Times, 25

looters: fears of, 21, 32, 41; items taken by, 24; media misrepresentation of, 22, 23, 24, 25, 26, 27, 28–29, 32; official misrepresentation of, 23, 25, 38, 42; police as, 23; sign against, 22

Los Angeles Times, 26, 30

Louisiana, ix, x, 3–4, 5, 7, 8, 9, 18, 21, 23, 49–50, 51, 53, 61, 66, 69, 75, 96, 103, 107, 130n18. See also New Orleans; Plaquemines Parish; wetlands

Louisiana Department of Wildlife and Fisheries, 19, 21, 52

Lower Ninth Ward, 61, 62

Lower Ninth Ward residents: Katrina flooding experienced by, 75, 84; racism suspected by, 75, 129n10; restoration for, 61, 62

low-income residents, 71; disasters affecting, xiv, 74–75; discrimination against, 63, 66; Katrina affecting, xiv, 75

marshland, 8, 50

media: on axes, 83; color line of, 24–25; evolution of, x, 12–13, 21; on federal disaster response, 18–19; Limbaugh as, 42; misinformation spread by, 22–23, 25–27, 35, 38; narrative of, xii, 117n2; on New Orleans, 11; oversight, 43; racial inequality captured by, 87–88; reconsideration by, 27–30, 124n94; on survivors, 16; in US, 29. See also journalists

mental illness, 58–59

meteorologists, 12

Miami Herald, 26

Michigan State troopers, 63

migrations, 95–96, 97, 99

military troops: at Convention Center, 37; deadly force threat of, 34;

64, 100; White flight of, 15–16; White vigilantes among, 45, 46

New Orleans Times-Picayune, 4

New York Daily News, 26

New York Times: acknowledgment by, 30; misinformation spread by, 22, 38; "More Horrible Than Truth" in, 27; "Superdome" in, 40

9/11 evacuation, 45

911 call center, 82–83

Ninth Ward, 58. *See also* Lower Ninth Ward

nursing homes, 118n22

officials: displacement decision by, xiv–xv, 96; evacuation stance of, 80, 81; perspective of, 43; response failure of, 18, 80, 86–87; volunteers blocked by, 21

oil spills, 5

Pardee, Jessica, 39–40

PBS NewsHour, 28

Penner, D'Ann, 34–35

Peterson, Jesse Jay, 79

pets, 13, 84

Plaquemines Parish: home destruction in, 7–8; resiliency of, 9–10

Point Algiers, 46

police: displaced persons blocked by, 44–45; as looters, 23; racism of, 63; shootings by, 45–46; and suicide attempt, 57

post-traumatic stress disorder (PTSD), 59, 92–93

poverty, xii, 16, 59, 62, 75, 78, 86, 91, 100, 105

prison, 127n10, 130 n18

prisoners, 18

PTSD. *See* post-traumatic stress disorder

public housing: demolition of, 65, 65–66, 67, 68; structural racism affecting, 65, 65, 66, 67, 67

race, of survivors, 89

racial divide, 44, 107

racial inequality: Black New Orleans residents affected by, 90–91; economic inequality combined with,

91; media capturing, 87–88; New Orleans residents affected by, 16

racial stereotyping, 43–44, 124n94

racial tension, 32, 43

racism: against displaced persons, 63; Lower Ninth Ward residents suspecting, 75, 129n10; of military troops, 35; against New Orleans residents, Black, 41–42, 64; of New Orleans residents, White, 41–42, 64, 100; of police, 63. *See also* structural racism

Reckdahl, Katy, 60

recovery, 11, 56, 57, 60, 61, 63, 66–67, 99, 101, 102, 106

refugees, 26, 31, 34, 35

reporters. *See* journalists; media

rescue efforts: by boat, 19, 20, 21, 86; with flotation devices, 120n34. *See also* humanitarian aid

residents. *See* Gulf Coast residents; Lower Ninth Ward residents; low-income residents; New Orleans residents; New Orleans residents, Black; New Orleans residents, White

resiliency, of Gulf Coast residents, 9–10

restoration, 106; funds for, 62; for Lower Ninth Ward residents, 61, 62

Rivlin, Gary, 24, 63

Road Home program, 126n26

saltwater, 53–54, 126n21

Scheper-Hughes, Nancy, 45

school buildings, 7, 49, 100

school system, 66; and charter experiment, 66; desegregation of, 15–16; and racial segregation, 16, 66, 91

sea level, 14

sediment, 49–50, 55

settlements, human, ix–x, 3–4; inequality vulnerability of, 74; nature reshaped by, 50–51

shootings, 45–46; fears of, 35; rumors of, 25, 29, 39, 41, 42; threats of, 23, 34, 41

social science, ii, xi, xiii, 7, 61, 73, 74, 76, 77, 79, 85, 92, 93, 94, 105, 106, 123n89, 127n10

Stack, Carol, 79

Standing in the Need (Browne), 102
St. Bernard Parish, 57, 118n22; barricade in, 32, *33*; racial tension in, 32
storm surge: from hurricanes, xiii; from Katrina, ix, 3, 4, 6, 10, 54, 82; in Industrial Canal, 15, 51; in MRGO, 15, 51, 53, 55
stress, as terminology, 92–93
structural racism, 126n26; Charity Hospital affected by, 66; diaspora permanence from, 63–66, 67, 68; against displaced persons, 63–64, 65, *65*, 66–67, *67*, 68; of New Orleans city leaders, 63–64, 65, *65*, 66–67, *67*; against New Orleans residents, Black, 63–64, 65, *65*, 66–67, *67*, 68, 130n18; public housing affected by, 65, *65*, 66, 67, *67*; results of, 68; school system affected by, 66; voting rights affected by, 64–65
suicide, 57; contemplation of, 84, 85; as fatality, 30, 56–57
Superdome: fatality count at, 30; military troops arrival at, 37; misinformation about, 25, 28, 29, 30, 34, 37, 39, 40–41, 44, 45; survivors at, 16, 78, 86, 88
"Superdome" (Treaster), 40
support systems: and Covid-19 pandemic isolating, 108; for New Orleans families, 98, 101, 129n12
survivors, *17*; absence of, 4; agencies' disconnect with, 101–102; at Convention Center, 16, 123n84; disaster personification of, 73–74; disorientation of, 7–8; family structure of, 78; of Holocaust, 93; Jackson on, 16; journalists on, 86, 89; Katrina flood stranding, 83–84, 85, 88–89, *89*; media on, 16; Ninth Ward evacuation of, *58*; race of, 89; rescue efforts for, 19, *20*, 21, 86, 120n34; at Superdome, 16, *88*; trauma of, xiii, 59–60, 71, 94, 103. *See also* firsthand accounts

Texas, 96, 100
Thevenot, Brian, 28, 44, 124n94

Thibodeaux, Jacques, 29, 37
Tierney, Kathleen, 23, 32
Times-Picayune: on military troop findings, 37; on police shootings, 45; professionalism failing at, 28, 30; on racial stereotyping, 44
Toussaint, Harold, 34–35
trauma: accumulation of, 75, 93; definition of, 91–92; from human failure, 11, 33; misinformation influenced by, 39–41; of survivors, xiii, 59–60, 71, 94, 103. *See also* firsthand accounts; post-traumatic stress disorder
Treaster, Joseph B., 40
trees, 6–7; cypress, 53, 55

United States: displaced persons in, 95–96; family in, 76–78; media in, 29; New Orleans media attention in, 11; oil spills in, 5; racial divide in, 44, 107
US Army Corps of Engineers, 55

vehicles, 17, 25, 27, *33*, 79, 118n16
Voting Rights Act (1965), 64–65
vulnerable populations, xiv, xv, 21, 58, 73, 74, 80–81, 86, 106, 129n5

Washington Post: acknowledgment by, 30; misinformation spread by, 22
wealthy persons, 16, 26, 64, 75, 91
Weber, Daniel, 85
West, Kanye, 24
wetlands: as buffer zone, 50; disappearance of, 54–55; engineering of, 51; fossil fuel disruption of, 51–52; livelihoods in, 9; plants in, 50, 53; productivity of, 8–9; saltwater harming, 53–54; vulnerability of, 8, 13–14
White flight, 15–16
White vigilantes, 45, 46
Will, George, 78–79
women, as New Orleans family leaders, 57, 101, 103